LEARN TO MAKE
CHILDREN'S CLOTHES

Sue Locke

THE MAIN STREET PRESS ● PITTSTOWN, NEW JERSEY

*To Tim, my husband, for his constant support
and encouragement and to our children, Simon
and Samantha, for being an inspiration for my
designs, and such patient models*

*The author thanks the following companies for their
help in the preparation of this book:
Scovill Dritz, for press-on fasteners and dressmakers'
squared paper
John Lewis Partnership, for fabrics (pages 20, 26, 45)
Viyella, for fabric (page 36)
Mothercare and Hennes, for accessories*

First American Edition 1987

Copyright © 1987 by Sue Locke

Published by
The Main Street Press, Inc.
William Case House
Pittstown, New Jersey 08867

Published originally by
William Collins Sons & Co Ltd
London, England

Designed and produced by TL Creative Services
Series Editor Eve Harlow
Illustrated by Terry Evans and John Hutchinson
Photography by Tim Bishopp

Printed by New Interlitho, Italy

Library of Congress Cataloging-in-Publication Data

Locke, Sue.
Learn to make children's clothes.
1. Children's clothing.   I. Title.
TT635.L59   1987   646.4'06   86-33168

ISBN 1-55562-014-0

Contents

1 Learning to Sew

2 Baby Wardrobe

3 Toddler Wardrobe

4 Pre-School Wardrobe

Introduction

It is not easy to find clothes for children that are both original in design and inexpensive. And if you do find something you like, either the size or the colour you want may not be available.

After several tiring shopping trips for my baby son's wardrobe, I decided I would design and make his clothes myself. To my delight, I found I could complete a garment in an evening and, by sewing different fabrics, use a pattern again and again.

Many of my friends also have young children and they were so impressed with the results that I decided to show other mothers (and sisters, aunts and grandmothers), how easy making children's clothes can be.

I have tried to keep the sewing very simple. All the designs in this book have easy-to-

follow patterns, and no previous dressmaking experience or special skills are required to sew the clothes.

Several of the designs are constructed from squares and rectangles of fabric. Others have just two or three main pattern pieces. I have avoided buttons and buttonholes and used press-on fasteners instead. Only one pattern features a zip fastener, and I have used simple, plain seams throughout.

Making clothes for your children will undoubtedly save you money. I am sure you will also discover that making a new outfit is quicker — and far less exhausting — than trailing around the shops. Above all, you will have the pleasure of seeing your children wearing fashionable, flattering clothes that *fit,* knowing you have created them yourself.

Learning to Sew

Even if you have never tried dressmaking before you should be able to make the children's clothes in this book, provided you are prepared to learn the basic techniques described in this chapter. Read them carefully before starting any of the patterns – and then refer back as you work. The advice given here will provide the knowledge and confidence you need to succeed.

Patterns for dressmaking

Making clothes at home, whether for yourself or for children, involves the use of a pattern.

The children's clothes in this book are made from two types of pattern. In the first, you are given the measurements of pieces of fabric, and you use these to cut the fabric directly.

The other type is a graph pattern showing the pattern pieces reduced in size on a squared grid. To obtain a life-sized pattern, you copy the pattern pieces on to dressmakers' squared paper of the correct scale. All the graph patterns in this book are to a scale of 1 square of the grid representing 5cm (2in).

Making paper patterns

Making your own paper patterns from graph patterns is the first, basic stage in dressmaking. Making patterns is not difficult, and it helps you to recognise the various pieces of a garment, so that when you reach the stitching stage, you will feel confident about putting the garment together.

You need the following materials and equipment for pattern making:

● Dressmakers' squared paper to the specified scale. (If squared paper is not easily available, make your own by taping large sheets of wrapping paper together and then measure and rule squares as required.)
● Tape measure and ruler
● Medium-soft pencils
● Scissors for cutting paper. (Always keep a pair of scissors specially for cutting paper. Once used for this purpose, they are virtually useless for cutting anything else.)

A flexible plastic ruler is useful for drawing curves (obtainable from art shops) but is not essential.

Study the graph pattern and count the number of squares, first across the top edge and then down one side. This tells you the dimensions of squared paper you need to make the pattern.

With a pencil, number the squares on the graph pattern, across the top edge and then down one side (Fig 1). Now number the squares on the squared pattern paper in the same way.

Using a ruler, and working from the graph pattern, draw the straight lines of the pattern. Then, still working from the graph pattern, mark crosses at key points on the curved lines (Fig 2). Join up the crosses to complete the outline of pattern pieces.

Pattern sizes and markings

Most of the patterns in this book are given in two sizes. The smaller size is shown on the graph pattern in a coloured line. Make sure you draw the pattern size required.

The patterns bought from shops are printed with lines, words and symbols to help you in cutting out

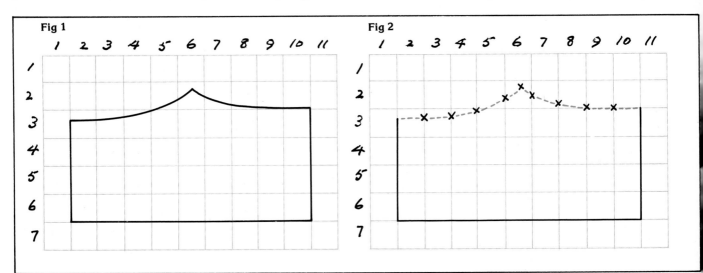

Fig 1 *Number the squares on the graph pattern, across the top edge and then down one side*

Fig 2 *Draw the straight lines of the pattern on to squared paper, then mark crosses at key points on the curved lines*

and assembling the garment. The patterns in this book are simplified and use only a few lines, words, letters and symbols.

Before using the pattern, copy all the lines, words, symbols and letters from the graph pattern. The markings are essential information to help you in making up the garment.

Fig 1 shows the various markings on patterns.

Fig 1 *Get to know pattern markings before attempting a project*

Fabrics and materials

The pattern instructions in the following chapters include the materials required for making each garment. A choice of fabrics is usually given, and it is important to follow the recommendations, since fabrics have been selected as being suitable for the child's age-group, easy to work with, comparatively inexpensive and machine-washable.

Sometimes, a substitute fabric is recommended. For instance, some babies are allergic to wool, in which case a brushed cotton is a recommended substitute for clothes that are worn next to the skin.

Alternative fabrics are also given for different seasons, such as poly/cotton for a summer garment and needlecord or denim for a winter version.

Fabric quantities

Alongside the recommended fabric is the amount you need to make the garment, expressed in terms of length and width.

When purchasing fabric from a bolt or roll, you will find the width marked on a label. The width is the measurement across the fabric from one selvedge (the finished edge) to the other.

Buy the length of fabric recommended and the correct width,

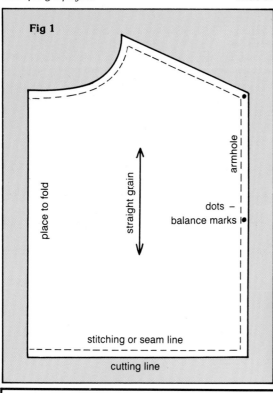

Sizes chart

The chart indicates the approximate measurements of babies and children in age-groups, from six months to five years old. However, children do not necessarily conform to these sizes and you are advised to check the child's measurements before using the patterns in this book.

	Chest	Waist	Approximate height
Babies			
6–12 months	48cm *(19in)*	48cm *(19in)*	70cm *(28in)*
12–18 months	50cm *(20in)*	49cm *(19½in)*	80cm *(31in)*
Toddlers			
1½–2 years	53cm *(21in)*	50cm *(20in)*	90cm *(35½in)*
2–3 years	56cm *(22in)*	52cm *(20½in)*	97cm *(38in)*
Pre-school children			
3–4 years	58cm *(23in)*	53cm *(21in)*	104cm *(41in)*
4–5 years	60cm *(24in)*	55cm *(21½in)*	112cm *(44in)*

to ensure that all the pattern pieces can be cut from the fabric.

Children's clothes use very little fabric and you may be tempted to shop for sale remnants. Always take a tape measure with you and check both the length and width of the remnant to ensure that it is sufficient for the pattern.

Fabric layouts

A guide to laying out pattern pieces of fabric is given with the graph patterns in this book. Follow these layouts carefully when pinning the pattern pieces to fabric, taking careful note of grain lines and of those pieces that are to be cut out on the fold of fabric (see Fig 1).

Sewing equipment

Only a few items of equipment are needed initially, but you will probably add to your work basket as you become more experienced.

Here are your basic requirements:
- Sewing-machine with both straight and zigzag stitch facilities
- Dressmakers' shears with long blades, for cutting fabric
- A pair of small, sharp scissors, for trimming, cutting threads, etc
- A pair of pinking shears (with serrated blades), for trimming seams
- A piece of tailors' chalk (or, if preferred, dressmakers' carbon paper and a tracing wheel), for marking fabric
- A tape measure, dressmakers' steel pins, a seam ripper (for unpicking machine-stitching)
- A bodkin or safety pin, for threading elastic into casings
- Needles (It is worth buying a mixed pack of hand-sewing needles.)
- Threads (Choose a multi-purpose thread, such as Coats Drima, for hand-sewing. Use basting thread for basting.)

Always make sure that pins have been removed from fabric or partially finished garments before fitting on children. A hidden pin can scratch badly. Wherever possible, use small safety pins for holding pieces in place when fitting on a child.

Make absolutely sure that no pins have been left in seams when finishing seam edges.

Before you sew

Having drawn out the paper pattern and copied all the lines and marks from the graph pattern, cut out the pattern pieces.

1. Press any creases from the fabric and spread it on a flat surface (a table top or uncarpeted floor) with selvedges together (Fig 2). The right side of the fabric is inside the fold.
2. Referring to the fabric layout, lay the pattern pieces on the fabric, taking special note of those pieces that are to be cut on the fold of the fabric. Check that the grain line on the pattern pieces lies along the straight grain of fabric.

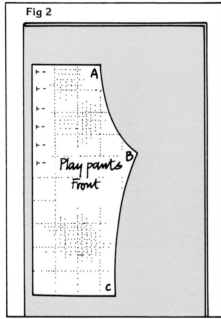

Fig 2 *Set pins across the seam allowance about 2.5-3cm (1-1¼in) apart*

3. Pin the pattern pieces to the fabric, setting pins across the seam allowance and about 2.5-3cm (1-1¼in) apart (see Fig 2). Pick up only a small amount of both layers of fabric as you pin.

Cutting out

4. Begin with the largest pattern pieces. Hold the shears with the large blade underneath and cut round the pattern pieces, using long, slow strokes. Cut out all the pattern pieces but do not unpin the paper pattern at this stage. Put all the fabric scraps on one side.

Transferring marks

5. Using tailors' chalk, mark in the letters and dots you need to match pattern pieces, such as on shoulder seams, side seams, collars and necklines (see Fig 1).

If you prefer to use dressmakers' carbon paper and a tracing wheel, position the carbon paper, coloured side down, between the fabric and the paper pattern and mark with a tracing wheel or a blunt pencil.
6. Unpin the paper pattern and keep the pieces by you to refer to as you work.

Stitching seams

Your sewing-machine's manual will tell you how to thread it and fill the bobbin. Check that you have the correct needle for the fabric with which you are working. Test the stitch before starting to sew. Fold a scrap of the fabric and work a few stitches through the doubled fabric. Your manual will tell you what to do if the resulting stitch is less than perfect.

All the garments in this book are stitched using plain seams. To work this type of seam, proceed as follows:
1. Place two fabric pieces together with right sides facing and any markings matching. The cut edges of fabric should be together. Pin the two pieces of fabric together, setting pins across the seam line (Fig 3, this page). Pins should be about 2.5-3cm (1-1¼in) apart.
2. Work basting stitches just inside the seam line, about 1.5mm (¹/₁₆in) away.
3. Machine-stitch along the seam

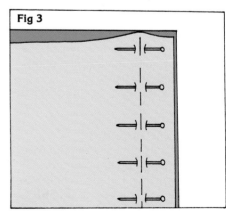

Fig 3 *Pin the two pieces of fabric together, right sides facing, setting pins across the seam line. Baste just outside the seam line*

line. For the patterns in this book the seam allowance is 1cm (⅜in), so stitch 1cm (⅜in) from the cut edges of fabric (Fig 1).

4. Finish off the thread ends as described under Seam Finishes.

5. Unpick the basting stitches.

6. Press the seam flat first, then open it with your fingers and press the seam open, along the stitching line. This helps to 'set' the stitches (see Pressing on page 11).

7. Finish the seam by neatening the raw edges of the seam allowances by one of the methods described here.

Seam finishes

Your machine-stitching will be stronger and less likely to become undone if each line of stitching is finished properly.

Start and finish a seam by running the machine back for 6mm (¼in), then running it forward. Knot the thread ends together and trim them short. If the stitching line ends before the edge of the fabric, pull the thread end on the underside of the work until the top thread loop comes through. Pull the loop and the top thread will come through. Tie the thread ends together tightly and trim the ends short.

Neatening seam allowances

The cut edges of seam allowance are neatened to prevent them from fraying. There are various ways of doing this but, for the patterns in this book, the following simple techniques are recommended.

Pinked Machine-stitch the seam, then press the seam allowance open. Trim the seam edges with pinking shears. This is suitable for fabrics that do not fray easily (Fig 2).

Zigzagged Machine-stitch and then press the seam open. Work machine zigzag stitch along the cut edges of the seam allowance (Fig 3).

Narrow seams On some of the

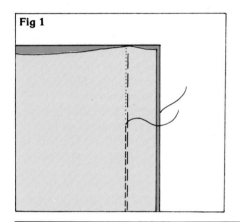

Fig 1

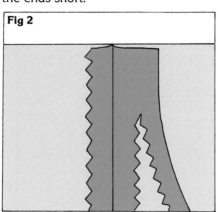

Fig 2

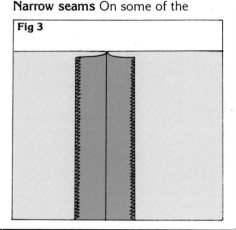

Fig 3

Hand-sewing stitches

In all dressmaking, a certain amount of hand-sewing is required. Although your sewing-machine takes the hard work out of the job, hand-sewing can be the final touch of good finish and should not be underestimated.

Before sewing-machines were invented, clothes were stitched together by hand and seams were joined with fine running stitches. If a sewing-machine is not available to you, there is no reason why you should not make the designs in this book entirely by hand.

Here are the hand-sewing stitches you need.

Basting (or tacking)

These stitches are used to hold two pieces of fabric together temporarily and also provide a guide to help you to achieve a straight seam (Fig 7).

Running stitch

Running stitch has many uses in

dressmaking (Fig 8). It is used in this book for gathering fabric (see page 10 for technique).

Backstitch

Some children's clothes can be made without the help of a sewing-machine, and backstitch is used for working seams. It is a strong, hard-wearing stitch and, properly worked, looks very like machine-stitching (Fig 9).

Hemming

Hemming, as its name suggests, is used to hold hems in place (Fig 10).

Slipstitch

Slipstitches (sometimes called slip hemming) are used to join two folded edges invisibly, on hems and for attaching trims (Fig 11).

Oversewing

Oversewing, also called overcasting, is used on raw edges to prevent them fraying. It can be worked on seam allowances instead of machine zigzag stitches (Fig 12).

Fig 7 *Basting Begin with a double backstitch. Pick up 6mm (¼in)-long stitches on the needle, spacing them 6mm (¼in) apart*

Fig 8 *Running stitch Begin with a double backstitch. Pick up several tiny stitches on the needle, all of the same length, with the same amount of fabric between stitches*

Fig 9 *Backstitch Begin with a double stitch, then bring the needle through from the back of the work about 3mm (⅛in) forward along the seam line. Re-insert the needle about 3mm (⅛in) behind the point where the thread came through and bring it out again 3mm (⅛in) forward on the seam line. Continue, inserting the needle at the end of the last stitch and bringing it through 3mm (⅛in) ahead*

Fig 10 *Slipstitch Bring the needle through just under the folded edge of fabric. Slide the needle through the fold for about 6mm (¼in), then pick up a thread or two of the under fabric or adjacent fold*

Fig 11 *Hemming This stitch is usually made with the work held over the forefinger. Take a tiny stitch, then bring the needle up diagonally through the edge of the hem. Space stitches 6mm (¼in) apart*

Fig 12 *Oversewing This stitch can be worked from left to right or from right to left. Work diagonally-placed stitches over the raw edge, keeping them evenly spaced and all of the same depth*

garments in this book you will be instructed to trim the seam allowance back to 3mm (⅛in) to reduce bulk. This is done, for instance, when making a strap, before turning to the right side.

When the seam allowance is required to be a little narrower than usual – 6mm (¼in) – seams are neatened as follows. After machine-stitching, press the seam flat and then trim the seam allowance as instructed. Work zigzag stitch on the cut edges together, through both thicknesses of fabric. Press the seam to one side (Fig 4).

Curved seams, such as on trousers'

crotches, underarms and necklines, require to be clipped with scissors so that the fabric in the seam allowance can spread and lie flat. Clip almost up to the stitching line (Fig 5) but take care not to cut the stitches.

Reducing bulk Where two seams cross, for instance on trousers' crotches, there will be four layers of fabric. To reduce the bulk, trim the corners of the first seam made (Fig 6).

Fig 1 *Machine-stitch on the seam line, 1cm (⅜in) from the cut edge*

Fig 2 *Trim the seam allowance with pinking shears*

Fig 3 *Work zigzag stitches along the cut edges of the seam allowance*

Fig 4 *On narrow seams, trim the seam allowance back to 6mm (¼in) and work zigzag stitches through both seam allowances together*

Fig 5 *On curved seams, clip into the seam allowance*

Fig 6 *Where two seams cross, trim the corners of the first seam made to reduce bulk*

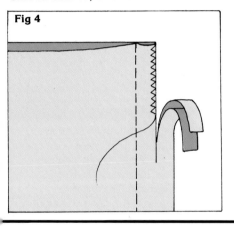

Fig 4

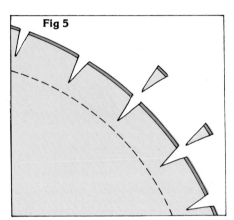

Fig 5

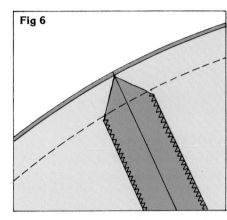

Fig 6

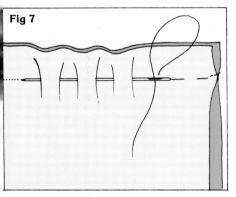

Fig 7

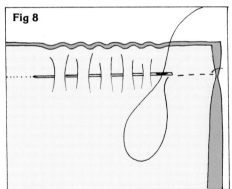

Fig 8

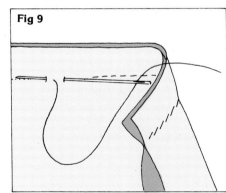

Fig 9

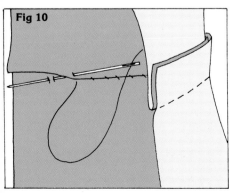

Fig 10

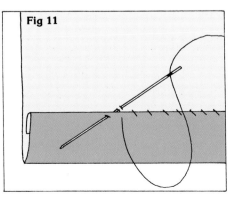

Fig 11

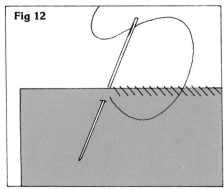

Fig 12

Gathering

Gathering can be done by hand or on a sewing-machine.

If it is being worked by hand, use small running stitches (see previous page, Fig 8). Start by securing the thread end with several backstitches. Pull up the needle to make gathers and wind the thread end in a figure-of-eight round a pin inserted vertically (Fig 1).

Machine-gathering is worked with the longest stitch available on the machine. Leave the thread ends long at both ends. At one end, wind both threads around a pin in a figure-of-eight and pull up the bobbin thread

Above: You will be using gathering techniques when making the Pyjama Suit (page 40) and the Country Style dress (page 48)

at the other. Wind this round a pin also to hold the gathering.

Working gathered fabric

Unless otherwise instructed, two rows of gathering stitches are worked, to ensure an even finish.
1. Draw up the gathered fabric so that it is the same width as the piece to which it is being joined.
2. Pin the gathering to the fabric,

right sides facing, raw edges even, placing pins vertically between the folds (Fig 2). Work small basting stitches just below the gathering stitches. Remove the pins.
3. Machine-stitch from the gathered fabric side, working stitches on the seam line. When stitching, work slowly, and use the tips of a pair of scissors to arrange the folds ahead of the needle, so that they are not pushed along by the presser foot (Fig 3).
4. Leave gathering threads in place but remove basting stitches.
5. Trim the seam allowances by 3mm (⅛in) and work zigzag stitches over the edges of fabric.

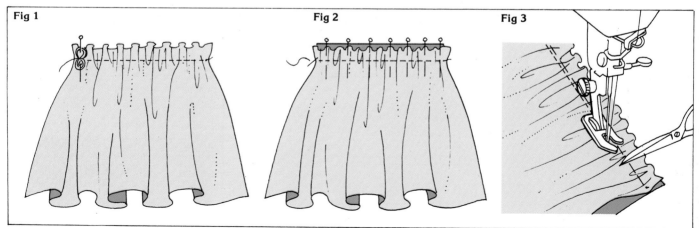

Fig 1 *Pull up gathering thread and twist round a pin inserted vertically*

Fig 2 *Set pins across the seam allowance between the gathers*

Fig 3 *Use scissor points to prepare gathers for the machine foot*

Pressing

As any experienced dressmaker will tell you, pressing is an essential part of dressmaking. Always keep the ironing board up and an iron and pressing cloth ready when you are sewing and press every seam as soon as it has been stitched, to give a professional finish to your work.

It is important to note that pressing is different from ironing. To press, the iron is set down, lifted, and set down again, along the seam, until the seam is completed. Always test the heat of the iron on a scrap of the fabric to prevent accidental scorching.

Pressing a seam

After stitching has been completed, remove the basting threads. Press the seam flat. Open the seam allowances with your fingers and press again along the seam line. (In some patterns, you will be instructed to press seam allowances to one side.)

Pressing gathers

When pressing gathered fabric, use the point of the iron, working between the folds and towards the stitches.

Bias binding

On some of the patterns in this book bias binding is used to finish a raw edge. Some designs use ready-made binding, while others use bias strips cut from left-over fabric.

Cutting bias strips

1. Trim the ends of fabric so that they are straight to the grain. Fold one end diagonally, with the cut edge against the selvedge to find the true bias. Mark the fold with a chalk line (Fig 4).
2. Open out the fabric and, using a ruler, mark lines parallel to the chalked line and to the width specified in the pattern instructions (Fig 5).
3. Cut the strips. If strips require to be joined to obtain a length, place two strips at right angles, right sides together (Fig 6). Machine-stitch. Open out and press (Fig 7). Trim the protruding corners of the seam allowance.
4. Fold bias strips lengthwise, cut

edges to the centre and wrong sides facing, and press before applying (Fig 8).

Applying bias strips

Ready-made bias binding has the edges already folded to the wrong side. The method used for applying ready-made bias binding and bias strips you cut yourself is basically the same.
1. Open the bias binding and, with right sides together and raw edges even, pin the binding along the garment edge (Fig 9).
2. Baste just below the seam line, then remove the pins. Machine-stitch on the seam line. Remove basting.
3. Turn the bias binding over to the wrong side of work, folding in ends. Slipstitch to the seam line (Fig 10).

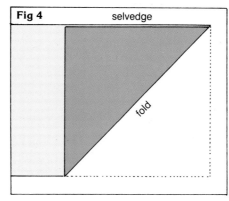

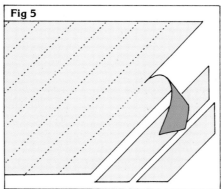

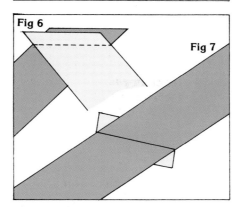

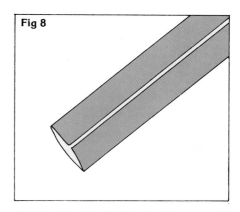

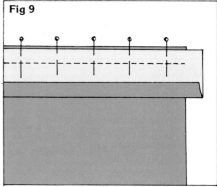

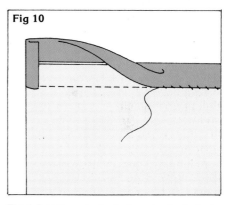

Fig 4 *Fold the cut edge to the selvedge to find the true bias*

Fig 5 *Mark lines parallel to the bias fold line*

Fig 6 *Place two pieces at right angles and machine-stitch*

Fig 7 *Open the strip and press, trimming off points*

Fig 8 *Prepare bias strips for applying by pressing the long edges to the centre*

Fig 9 *Pin bias binding to the garment edge, right sides together, and baste just below the seam line*

Fig 10 *Turn bias binding to the wrong side and slipstitch along the seam line*

Casings

Casings are sewn along the edge of a garment to take a drawstring or elastic. Make a simple casing for children's clothes as follows:

1. Trim the fabric edge straight. Measure and mark with chalk the depth of casing required.
2. Work zigzag machine-stitching along the raw edge of fabric (Fig 1).
3. Turn the casing to the inside of the garment and machine-stitch 3mm (⅛in) from the neatened edge. Leave a 5cm (2in) gap in the stitching at the centre back seam for inserting elastic (Fig 2).

Inserting elastic

4. Cut a piece of elastic to the waist measurement, held loosely. Fasten one end with a safety pin inside the open casing on the centre back seam allowance. Slip another safety pin on the other end (Fig 3).
5. Ease the pin, with the elastic, through the casing. Pin the two ends together and try on the garment. Adjust the fit and overlap the elastic ends 12mm (½in). Cut off any surplus elastic.

6. Oversew the edges of the elastic together (Fig 4). Close the casing with machine-stitching.

Tip It is a good idea to mark the centre back seam on children's trousers with coloured thread so that you know the position of the join in the elastic, for possible replacement.

Applied casings

A casing for elastic or drawstrings can also be made by applying bias binding, wide tape or a strip of fabric to the garment. Applied casings can be worked on the inside of a garment, such as on trousers or skirts, or they can be worked on the outside of a dress or jacket for a decorative effect.

Applied casings using bias binding

1. Cut the garment edge straight and press a 12mm (½in) hem to the inside. Baste.
2. Cut a piece of bias binding to the waistline measurement plus 2.5cm (1in).
3. Pin and baste the binding to the garment, with the inside fold of binding to the right side of the turned hem (Fig 5), starting and ending at the centre back seam and

turning the ends under.
4. Baste the lower edge of the bias binding to the inside of the garment, then machine-stitch 3mm (⅛in) from the folded edges (Fig 6).
5. Insert elastic or a drawstring through the gap in the binding at centre back, using the same technique as for inserting elastic into a casing. Close the gap with slipstitches.

Fabric casings If casings are to be made from fabric, cut strips on the straight grain to the desired length plus 12mm (½in) and to the desired depth plus 12mm (½in). Turn and press 6mm (¼in) hems to the wrong sides on all edges. Use the strips as described for bias binding casings.

Fig 1 Mark the fold line for the casing and neaten the raw edge with zigzag stitching

Fig 2 Turn the casing to the inside and machine-stitch, leaving a gap in the seam

Fig 3 Fasten one end of the elastic with a safety pin to the centre back seam allowance

Fig 4 Join the overlapped elastic ends with oversewing all round

Fig 5 Baste bias binding over the edge of the turned hem, starting at the centre back seam

Fig 6 Machine-stitch on both edges

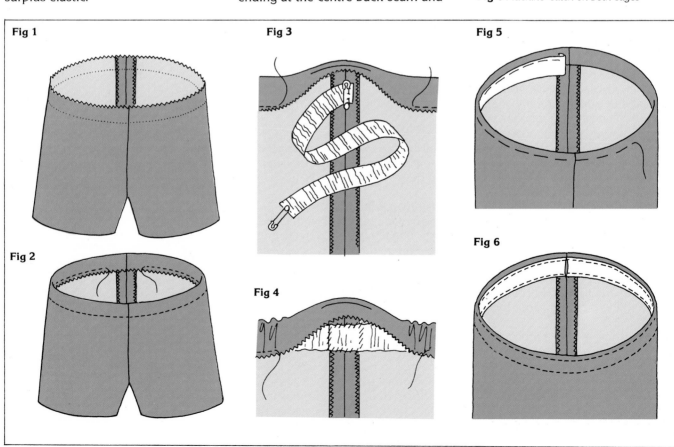

Fig 1

Fig 2

Fig 3

Fig 4

Fig 5

Fig 6

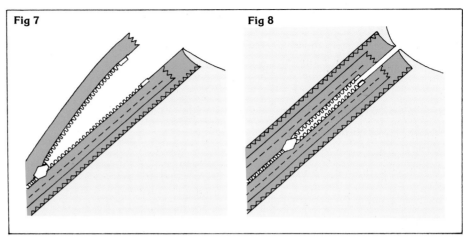

Fastenings

In many of the designs in this book, press-on fasteners are used. These are simple to apply and a good range of decorative styles is obtainable.

Press-on fasteners are sold in packs containing 6-10 fasteners, together with a tool for applying them and full instructions.

Zip fasteners

Zips are a practical fastener for some children's clothes and can be a decorative feature.

There are established methods for inserting different kinds of zips into garments. The following method is a simple version, which can be used on the denim jacket pictured above (see page 42 for pattern instructions).

You will find that it is easier to insert a zip before sections are seamed to the rest of the garment.
1. Press a 6mm (¼in) hem to the wrong side on the two garment sections.
2. Lay the sections wrong side up. Open the zip and place it so that the inner edge of the zip is aligned with the fold line of the fabric (Fig 7), and 12mm (½in) from the neck edge.
3. Baste the zip tape to the fabric. Using the zipper foot on the sewing-machine, machine-stitch close to the teeth.
4. Close the zip. Lay the folded edge of the other section along the teeth and baste.
5. Open the zip and machine-stitch, close to the teeth (Fig 8).
6. Catch the seam allowance to the tape edges on the wrong side to neaten.

Fig 7 *Align the inner edge of the zip along the fold and machine-stitch close to the teeth*

Fig 8 *Close the zip to position the opposite side. Open the zip to machine-stitch close to the teeth*

Fig 9 *Machine-stitch folded bias strip on the wrong side, then thread the ends into a large-eyed needle*

Fig 10 *Turn rouleau to the right side with needle and thread*

Fig 11 *Set rouleau loops across the opening and machine-stitch to the wrong side of the garment*

Button loops

Button loops are made with a narrow tube of fabric called 'rouleau'. To make button loop rouleau, cut bias strips 3.5cm (1¼in) wide. The length of the strip depends on how many loops are required.
1. Fold the strip in half lengthwise, right sides facing, and machine-stitch, leaving the ends open.
2. Leave a long length of the machine's threads hanging. Trim the seam allowance back to 3mm (⅛in). Thread the ends into a large-eyed needle (Fig 9).
3. Make a backstitch at the end of the machine-stitching to secure the threads, then push the needle, eye first, into the tube (Fig 10).
4. Ease the needle through the tube and you will find that the threads pull the tube right side out. Cut the threads.
5. Do not press the rouleau tube. Cut the rouleau into lengths to fit over the button plus 2cm (¾in).
6. Sew or machine-stitch the loop to the inside of the garment, to correspond with the button (Fig 11).

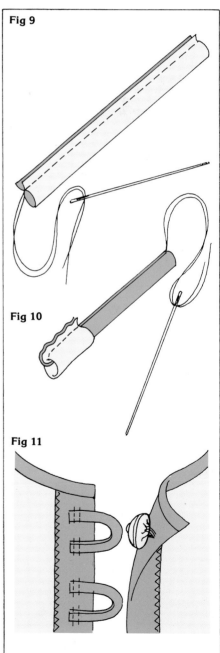

Fig 7

Fig 8

Fig 9

Fig 10

Fig 11

Cuffs and hems

Sleeve ends, skirt hems and the hems on trouser legs can be finished in different ways, depending on the amount of wear the garment receives.

Pinked and stitched hem

This hem is quick to do and is usually used on hems with little wear, such as cuffs and sleeve ends.

1. Trim the fabric edge straight. Measure the hem to be turned and mark with a chalk line on the right side of fabric. Fold and press the hem.
2. Trim the cut edge with pinking shears. Machine-stitch 3mm *(⅛in)* from the pinked edge (Fig 1).

Turned-under hem

This hem wears well and looks neat from the inside of the garment. Use it on skirt and trouser hems.

1. Trim the fabric edge straight and measure and mark the depth of hem on the right side.
2. Turn and press a narrow 6mm *(¼in)* hem to the wrong side on the cut edge. This is best done in one action on the ironing board, turning the hem with your fingers and pressing as you go.
3. Turn and baste the hem, folding on the marked line. Machine-stitch (Fig 2).

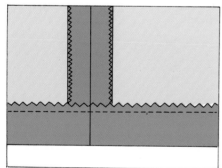

Fig 1 *Pinked and stitched hem*

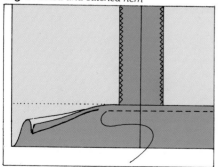

Fig 2 *Turned-under hem*

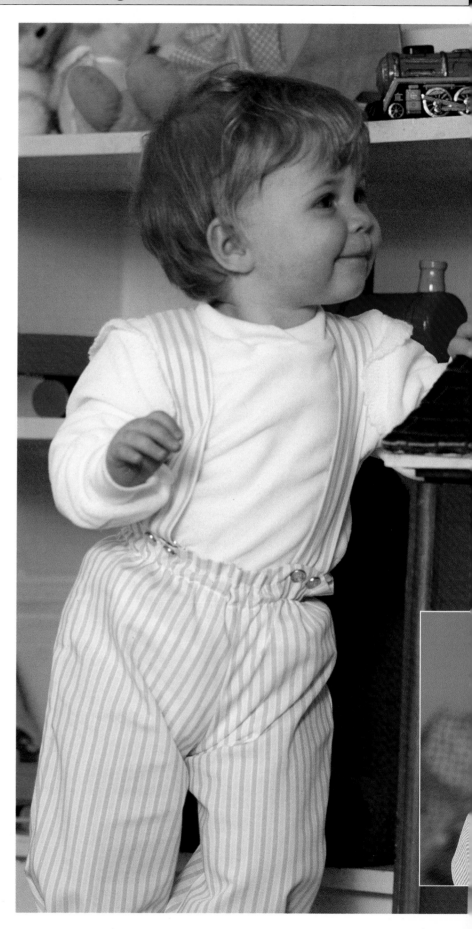

Straps, tabs, ties and belts

Some of the clothes in this book feature straps, tabs, ties and belts made from fabric (see straps and bow-tie pictured left). The technique for making all these is the same.

1. Fold the piece of fabric along its length, right sides facing. Baste on the long open side and one short end.
2. Machine-stitch, taking 6mm (¼in) seams. Trim the seam allowance back to 3mm (⅛in) and cut off the corners (Fig 3).
3. Turn the strip right side out through the open end. You may find that a tool, such as a round-ended knife blade, helps to push the fabric through (Fig 4).
4. Press on the right side, turning the seam allowances of the open end to the inside. Slipstitch the open end or machine-stitch across to close (Fig 5).

Shaped straps

When two pieces of fabric are used to make a strap, for instance when shaped ends are required, proceed as follows:

1. Baste and machine-stitch two pieces together, right sides facing, leaving a gap in the middle of one long seam (Fig 6).
2. Turn to right side through gap. Press and close the open seam with slipstitches. This type of strap (or belt) is sometimes topstitched (Fig 7).

Fig 3 *Machine-stitch on one short end and long side, trim back seam allowance and cut off corners*

Fig 4 *Turn to right side through open end*

Fig 5 *Press, turn in open end and machine-stitch across to close*

Fig 6 *On shaped straps, machine-stitch two pieces together, right sides facing, leaving a gap in the seam on one long side*

Fig 7 *Press and close the open seam with slipstitches. This type of strap is sometimes also topstitched*

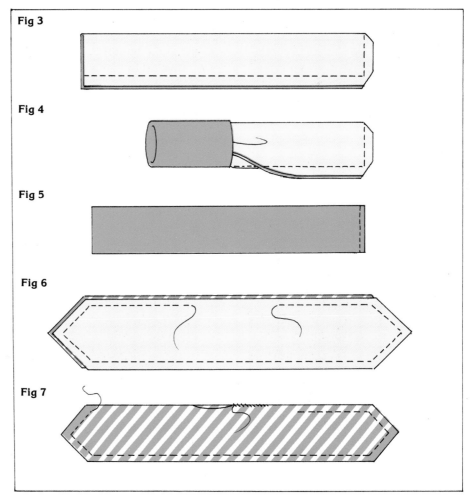

Fig 3

Fig 4

Fig 5

Fig 6

Fig 7

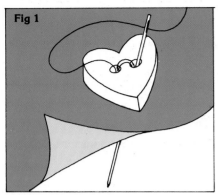

Fig 1 *Sew on button by bringing needle up through one hole, then pass it back down through the other hole. Repeat seven or eight times and finish thread off with several backstitches on the wrong side of the garment*

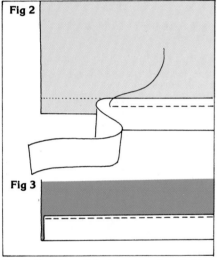

Fig 2 *Machine·stitch along one edge of ribbon positioned right side up on the wrong side of fabric edge*

Fig 3 *Fold ribbon over to the right side of fabric and machine·stitch the other edge*

Trims and decoration

You will find many ideas in this book for adding individual touches to children's clothes, using buttons, ribbons, braids, lace, etc, as well as appliquéd motifs.

Buttons

Children's buttons come in a vast range of novelty patterns. They can be used as mock fastenings, stitched to shoulder straps or to belts, or they can be used to make a bright and colourful decoration massed in one area or stitched at random on a garment. Sew buttons on firmly, securing threads with a double backstitch on the wrong side (Fig 1).

Ribbons and braids

Ribbons (and some braids) are available in washable polyester satins and grosgrains, some printed with designs and children's motifs. Ribbons can be used as ties and belts, as well as for colourful trimmings. They should be stitched to the garment pieces before joining the seams.

Use an iron·on ribbon bonding strip to position the ribbon before stitching both edges.

Ribboned edges Ribbon makes a good, hard·wearing finish for garment edges, such as skirt or trouser hems, cuffs, etc, and can also be used to edge frills and ruffles.

To apply ribbon, fold and press a turning less than the width of the ribbon to the right side of fabric. Open the turning flat and machine·

Lace to edge a skirt

stitch one edge of the ribbon, right side up, on the wrong side of the fabric, aligning the ribbon along the fold line (Fig 2). Turn the ribbon to the right side, along the fold, and stitch the other edge (Fig 3).

Ribbon ties If ribbon is being used for a neck bow or for a tie or belt, trim the ends off diagonally to minimise fraying.

Lace trims

Lace and broderie anglaise make very pretty trimmings for little girls' clothes, and add a delicate touch to baby clothes. Lace is available in various widths and a few colours, both in pre·gathered and plain

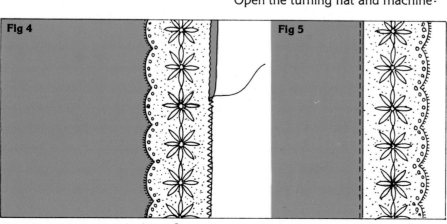

Fig 4 *Position lace, right sides facing, 3mm (⅛in) from the fabric edge. Work zigzag stitches from the lace heading edge and over the raw edge of fabric*

Fig 5 *Open the seam and stitch over the seam line from the right side of work*

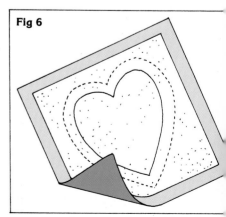

Fig 6 *Draw the motif on iron·on interfacing and iron interfacing to wrong side of fabric. Cut out the motif 6mm (¼in) from the drawn line*

Bias binding used for appliqué

styles. Polyester or polyester/cotton laces are recommended for children's clothes as these require no ironing and keep their freshness through launderings. Cotton lace can be dyed with multi-purpose dyes to match fabrics. Broderie anglaise is usually white or cream and made of washable cotton that may need light ironing after laundering.

Applying lace edging Spray-starch the lace and iron it. Place the lace along the raw edge of the fabric, right sides facing, with approximately 3mm (⅛in) of the fabric showing.

Set the sewing-machine to a close, narrow zigzag stitch. Work so that the stitch goes into the heading of the lace and then right off the fabric edge. Press the seam on the right side and work a very narrow line of zigzag stitching along the seam (Figs 4 and 5).

Appliqué

Appliqué is a delightful way of decorating children's clothes to give them an individual look. All kinds of ready-made motifs are available at sewing counters and in department stores. Some are iron-on while others need to be stitched on. (Before applying bought motifs to garments test that they are colourfast by pressing them under a damp cloth. Any colour bleed will immediately become apparent.)

Making appliqué motifs Appliqué motifs can be made from any small scraps of fabric left over from making children's garments. A single shape looks effective, or a small 'picture motif' can be worked with several pieces appliquéd together. Embroidery stitches can also be used on appliquéd motifs.

Working appliqué There are several ways of working appliqué but the following method is quick and easy and motifs will last through countless launderings.

1. Draw the motif on the non-adhesive side of lightweight iron-on interfacing. Iron the interfacing on to the fabric. Cut out the shape with 6mm (¼in) seam allowance all round (Fig 6).

2. Clip into the seam allowance almost up to the drawn line. Press the seam allowance to the wrong side (Fig 7).

3. Pin, then baste the motif to the fabric and work close zigzag stitch (satin stitch) over the motif edges (Fig 8).

If several motifs are being grouped together, baste all the pieces to the fabric first, then work zigzag stitching round the edges.

Decorative topstitching

Topstitching can be used as a decorative finish for clothes, emphasising the line of a garment. It is also used to keep seam edges flat. A heavy sewing thread can be used and a long machine stitch is recommended.

Stitch a plain seam and press the seam allowance to one side. Mark the topstitching line with tailors' chalk on the right side, the desired distance away from the seam and over the seam allowance (Fig 9).

Machine-stitch evenly from the right side of work, the stitches taking in the edges of the seam allowance on the wrong side (Fig 10).

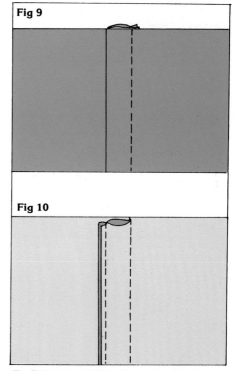

Fig 9 Work topstitching from the right side, through thicknesses of seam allowances pressed to one side

Fig 10 On the wrong side, topstitching catches in the edges of the seam allowance

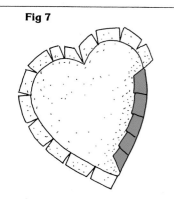

Fig 7 *Clip into the seam allowance, turning the allowance to the wrong side*

Fig 8 *With seam allowance pressed to the wrong side, baste the motif to the fabric and work close zigzag stitches over the edges*

Baby Wardrobe

Baby clothes should be easy to put on and take off, as well as comfortable for the child to wear. The clothes in this chapter, a snug baby suit, T-shaped top and play trousers, an all-in-one suit, sun-dress and party suit, are designed with these requirements in mind. Some of the garments can be worn together to make outfits, especially if the colour schemes pictured are followed.

Sun-dress

The Sun-dress is made very easily from two rectangular pieces of fabric. The skirt, which is worn high under the arms, is elasticated and can thus be adjusted as the baby grows. The shoulder straps fasten with press-on fasteners. The Sun-dress pictured is made of a summer-weight cotton but it could also be made in a heavier fabric, such as needlecord or wool, and teamed with a sweater for winter.

Materials required

To fit sizes chest 48-50cm (19-20in), length waist to hem 33cm (13in)

Pattern pieces Cut 2 Skirt pieces and 2 Straps from fabric

50cm *(20in)* of 91cm *(36in)*-wide cotton fabric

50cm *(20in)* of 2.5cm *(1in)*-wide cotton bias binding

50cm *(20in)* of 1cm *(⅜in)*-wide soft elastic

91cm *(36in)* of 6cm *(2½in)*-wide broderie anglaise edging

4 press-on fasteners

Matching sewing threads

Alternative fabrics Seersucker, poly/cotton, needlecord, wool and wool mixtures

Preparation

Cut 2 pieces 50cm *(20in)* wide and 34cm *(13½in)* long from the cotton fabric.

Cut 2 11cm *(4½in)*-long pieces from the broderie anglaise for pockets. Cut the remaining edging in 2 pieces for straps.

Working the design

1. Pin the 2 Skirt pieces together on the 34cm *(13½in)*-long side seams, right sides of fabric facing. Baste, then machine-stitch. Press seams open and neaten the edges.

Elasticated top edge

2. Measure and mark a line 2cm *(¾in)* down from the top edge of the skirt. Press a hem to the wrong side on this line.

Make an applied casing (see page 12), using bias binding (Fig 1).

3. Using a bodkin (or fasten a safety pin to the elastic end), thread elastic through the casing. Fasten the ends together with a safety pin while trying the skirt on the baby. Adjust the elastic for a comfortable fit.

Sew the elastic ends together (see page 12 for technique), and finish the casing seam.

Straps

4. Turn and press a narrow hem on the raw edges of both strap pieces. Turn and press a narrow hem on the short ends.

Turn a second, 2cm *(¾in)* hem on the long side of the straps and machine-stitch. The straps should now be about 3cm *(1⅛in)* wide.

5. Pin, baste and machine-stitch one end of the straps to the inside top edge of the Sun-dress, at the back and 10cm *(4in)* in from the side seams. Machine-stitch on the previous stitching lines of the casing

Fig 1 *Apply a casing of bias binding to the skirt, 12mm (½in) from the top edge*

Fig 2 *Machine-stitch the broderie anglaise straps to the inside top edge of the skirt, working over the stitching lines of the casing*

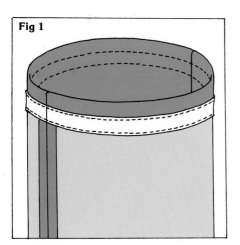

Fig 1

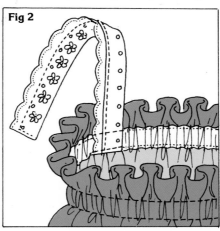

Fig 2

so that the elastic is not caught in the stitching (Fig 2).

Try the Sun-dress on the baby again and safety-pin the straps inside the front top edge of the skirt for a comfortable fit.

6. Attach press-on fasteners to the ends of the straps and to the front top edge of the skirt (see picture).

Hem and pockets

7. Make a turned-under hem, 2.5cm (1in) deep, on the bottom edge of the skirt (see page 14).

8. For the pockets, neaten the short ends and raw edges of both pocket pieces by turning and pressing a narrow hem to the wrong side.

9. Pin and baste the pockets to the skirt 5cm (2in) in from the side seams and aligning the straight edge of the pockets with the hem's stitching line (see picture). Topstitch the pockets in place (see page 17 for technique).

10. Attach a press-on fastener to both pockets.

Alterations to size

The fabric quantity given will also make a longer sun-dress. Cut the two skirt pieces to the desired length plus 3.5cm (1¼in) for the hem. The given top edge measurement – 50cm (20in) – will fit a bigger baby but adjust the elastic for a comfortable fit.

Frills and edgings

As the baby grows, the Sun-dress can be lengthened with a frill or a deep lace, or broderie anglaise, edging (Fig 3; see also page 17 for technique of applying lace edging).

Fig 3 *Join strips to make a frill, hemming the lower edge and gathering the top, pinked edge*

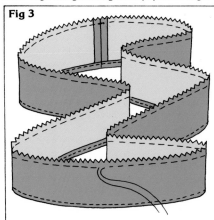

Fig 3

T-top

The loose-fitting T-top is made of easy-care white seersucker with contrasting bands of yellow bias binding. The back opening fastens with ties.

Materials required

To fit sizes chest 48-50cm (19-20in), sleeve length 15cm (6in)

Pattern pieces Front 1, Back 2, Sleeve 3

60cm *(24in)* of 91cm *(36in)*-wide seersucker fabric

3m *(3¼yd)* of 1cm *(⅜in)*-wide bias binding

Matching sewing threads

Alternative fabrics Poplin, lightweight denim, poly/cotton

Preparation

Fig 1 is the graph pattern for the T-top and the scale is 1 square=5cm *(2in)*. Two sizes are given on the pattern, the smaller size indicated in a coloured line. A seam allowance of 1cm *(⅜in)* is included on the pattern pieces.

Draw the pattern to scale on squared pattern paper and cut out the pieces, copying in all markings.

Following the fabric layout (Fig 2), pin the pattern pieces to fabric. Cut out 1 Front on the fold of fabric, 2 Backs and 2 Sleeves, transferring all markings.

Making the Top

1. Cut 2 strips of bias binding to fit from A–B and C–D (marked on pattern) and pin to the Front piece in position.
2. Cut 4 strips of bias binding to fit from E–F and G–H on the Sleeves. Pin in position.
3. Baste, then machine-stitch the strips, stitching on both edges.

4. Pin 2 Backs together, right sides of fabric facing, on the Centre Back seam from the bottom edge to the black dot on the pattern. Machine-stitch, then press the seam open.
5. Press back the seam allowances above the black dot and neaten the edges with pinking shears.

Joining Front to Back

6. Pin and baste the Front and Back together on the shoulder seams, right sides of fabric facing. Machine-stitch and press the seam open. Neaten the edges.

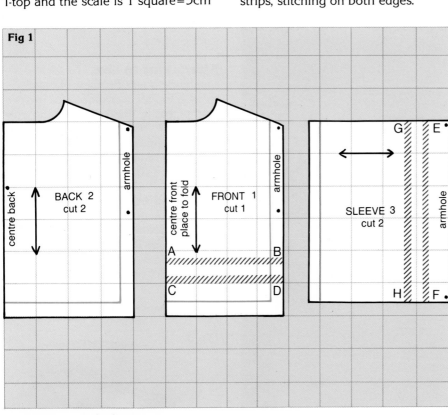

Fig 1 *Graph pattern for the T-top, 1sq=5cm (2in)*

Fig 2 *Fabric layout for the T-top*

Neck edge

7. Cut a piece of bias binding 84cm *(33in)* long and mark the middle with a pin. Matching the pin to Centre Front, bind the neck edge, leaving the ends of the binding to hang free at the back neck for ties (see page 11 for applying bias binding).
8. Fold, press and machine-stitch the binding ties, neatening the ends with hand-sewing (Fig 3).

Sleeves

9. Lay the garment flat, right side facing upwards, and pin the Sleeves along the edges marked 'armhole' (see pattern), matching the black dots. Baste the sleeves in position (Fig 4). Machine-stitch, press the seam open and then neaten the edges.

Underarm and side seams

10. Turn the Top inside out. Pin, then baste and machine-stitch the underarm and side seams in one operation, from the hem to the sleeve edge (Fig 5).
11. Clip into the underarm curve to ease the seam. Press the seam open and neaten the edges.
12. Trim the Sleeve ends with pinking shears. Turn and press a hem to the inside of the garment. Machine-stitch.
13. Make a turned-under hem on the bottom edge of the Top (see page 14), and press.

Fig 3 *Bind the neck edge, leaving ends for ties*

Fig 4 *Baste the sleeves along the armhole edges*

Fig 5 *Machine-stitch underarm and side seams*

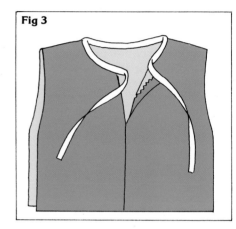
Fig 3

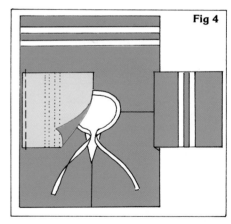
Fig 4

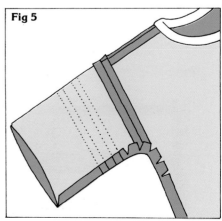
Fig 5

Play pants

These roomy, elastic-waisted trousers are perfect for playtime around the house, and could also be teamed with tops for more social occasions. The straps are fastened with pearl press-on fasteners, and matching fasteners are used on the smart ankle tabs.

Materials required
To fit sizes waist 48-50cm (19-20in), length waist to ankle 38-40cm (15-16in)

Pattern pieces Main piece 1. Cut 2 Straps and 2 Tabs from fabric

1m *(1⅛yd)* of 91cm *(36in)*-wide striped poly/cotton fabric

50cm *(20in)* of 1cm *(⅜in)*-wide soft elastic

50cm *(20in)* of 2.5cm *(1in)*-wide bias binding

6 pearl press-on fasteners

Matching sewing thread

Alternative fabrics Seersucker, lightweight woollen fabric

Preparation
Fig 1 is the graph pattern for the Play Pants. The scale is 1 square = 5cm *(2in)* and two sizes are given on the pattern, the smaller size indicated in a coloured line. A seam allowance of 1cm *(⅜in)* is included on the pattern.

Draw the pattern to scale on squared pattern paper. Cut out the pattern piece, copying in all markings.

Following the fabric layout (Fig 2), pin the pattern to the fabric and cut out 2 Fronts. Transfer markings and re-pin the pattern to cut out 2 Backs. Transfer markings.

From the remaining fabric, cut 2 ankle Tabs 9.5×11cm *(3¾ × 4½in)* and 2 Straps 52×10cm *(20½ × 4in)*.

Making the Pants
1. Pin 2 Fronts together on the Centre Front seam, right sides of fabric facing (A–B on pattern). Baste, then machine-stitch.

Clip into the curve to ease the seam (Fig 3). Press the seam open and neaten the edges.
2. Work the 2 Backs in the same way as for the Front.

Joining Front to Back
3. Pin Front to Back along the inside leg seams (B–C on pattern). Baste and then machine-stitch the seam in one operation, from C–B–C (on pattern). Clip into the curve to ease the seam, press seam allowance open and neaten the edges (Fig 4).

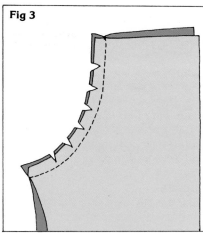

Fig 3 *Clip into the seam allowance after stitching the Centre Front seam*

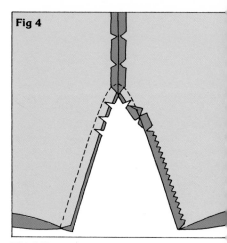

Fig 4 *The inside leg seam stitched, with the seam allowance clipped, the seam pressed open and neatened*

Side seams
4. Pin Front to Back on the side seams, right sides of fabric facing, then baste and machine-stitch. Press seams open and neaten.

Waist
5. Fold a 2cm *(¾in)* turning to the inside of the waist edge and work an applied casing using bias binding (see page 12 for technique).
6. Thread elastic through the casing and, after trying the Pants on the baby for fit, finish the elastic ends and close the seam in the casing.

Straps
7. Fold the Straps along the length, right sides facing, and make up the Straps (see page 15 for technique).
8. Pin the Straps to the inside back waist, positioning them 6.5cm *(2½in)* from the side seams, aligning the

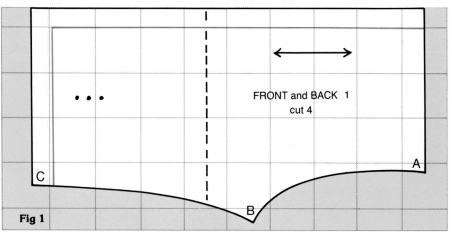

FRONT and BACK 1
cut 4

Fig 1

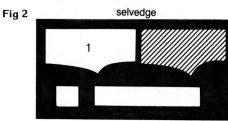

selvedge

1

fold

Fig 2

Fig 1 *Graph pattern for the Play Pants, 1sq = 5cm (2in). Use the pattern to cut 2 Fronts and 2 Backs*

Fig 2 *Fabric layout for the Play Pants. Cut out 2 Fronts, then re-pin the pattern to cut out 2 Backs*

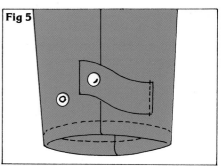

Fig 5 *Applying the ankle tab*

stitched edge of the Straps with the lower line of stitching on the casing. Machine-stitch the Straps in place, stitching over the previous lines of stitching on the casing, so that the elastic is not caught in.

9. Check the fit of the Straps on the baby and then apply two press-on fasteners to the ends of the front Straps and to the inside of the front waist, above the edge of the casing.

Ankle tabs

10. Make up the Tabs in the same way as for the Straps. Pin the stitched ends to the backs of the Pants legs, at the place marked on the pattern with three black dots. Topstitch in place.

11. Attach the top section of a press-on fastener to the other end of both Tabs.

12. Measure round the leg from the stitched end to the front, 7.5cm *(3in)*. Mark the place with chalk and then apply the other sections of the press-on fasteners (Fig 5).

13. Make a turned-under hem on the legs (see page 14) and press.

Alternative finish

If you prefer, make an elastic casing on the Pants' legs. After stage 4, turn a hem and machine-stitch (see page 12 for elastic casings).

Summer shorts

A pair of summer shorts can be made using the Play Pants pattern. Cut the paper pattern across the legs to the desired length and finish the hems with a turned-under hem (see page 14). Make the shorts in a bright, printed cotton or a soft towelling fabric.

The straps can be dispensed with altogether.

Party suit

This little suit has a long-sleeved top with a stand-up collar and bow-tie. The front is fastened with press-on fasteners. Make the trousers from the Play Pants pattern on page 24.

Materials required

To fit sizes chest 48-50cm (19-20in), waist 48-49cm (19-19½in), leg length 33-35cm (13-14in)

Pattern pieces Front 1, Back 2, Sleeve 3, Collar 4. Cut 1 piece of fabric for the bow-tie. Trousers from the Play Pants graph pattern on page 24

1.70m *(1⅞yd)* of 91cm *(36in)*-wide striped cotton fabric

40cm *(16in)* of 91cm *(36in)*-wide white cotton fabric

30×15cm *(12×6in)* piece of lightweight iron-on interfacing

5 press-on fasteners

50cm *(20in)* of 12mm *(½in)*-wide elastic

Alternative fabrics Poplin, lightweight denim, printed cotton

Preparation

Fig 1 is the graph pattern for the Party Suit Top. The scale is 1 square=5cm *(2in)* and two sizes are given on the pattern, the smaller size indicated in a coloured line. A seam allowance of 1cm *(⅜in)* is included on the pattern pieces.

Draw the pattern to scale on squared pattern paper and cut out the pieces, copying in all markings.

Following the fabric layout (Fig 2), pin the pattern pieces to the fabric and cut out 2 Fronts, 1 Back on the fold of the fabric, and 2 Sleeves. Transfer all markings.

The Collar is cut from white fabric, folded on the bias as shown in Fig 2. Cut a piece of white fabric 30×4.5cm *(12×1¾in)* for the bow-tie.

Use the Collar pattern to cut 1 piece from single thickness interfacing.

Trousers Draw a pattern from the graph pattern (Fig 1, page 24). Trim 2cm *(¾in)* from the pattern at the waist edge. Cut out the pieces and transfer markings. Pin the pattern to

fabric and cut out 2 Fronts and 2 Backs (see Fig 2, this page). Transfer all markings.

Making the Top

1. On both Front pieces, fold back the facings to the inside on the fold line marked on the pattern. Work two or three stitches to hold the fold at neck and bottom edges. Press the folds.

2. Pin the 2 Fronts to the Back on the shoulder seams, right sides of fabric facing. Baste and then machine-stitch the seams. Press open the seams and neaten the edges.

Collar

3. Trim 3mm *(⅛in)* all round the interfacing piece. Iron it to one side of the Collar piece, on the wrong side of fabric (Fig 3).

4. Re-fold the Collar, right sides of fabric facing, and machine-stitch the short ends, C–D on the pattern (Fig 4).

5. Trim the seam allowances back to

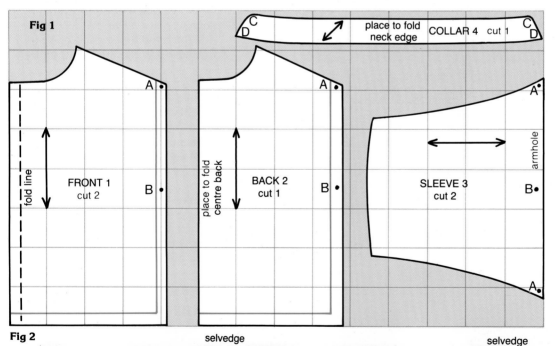

Fig 1 *Graph pattern for the Party Suit Top, 1sq=5cm (2in)*

Fig 2 *Fabric layout for the Party Suit*

3mm *(⅛in)* from the stitching. Turn the Collar right side out and press the edges.

6. Pin the Collar to the neckline, right side of the Collar to right side of the Top, matching the raw edges. Pin, setting pins vertically, then baste. Machine-stitch (Fig 5). Trim the seam allowance back to 6mm *(¼in)*.

7. Turning a 6mm *(¼in)* hem as you work, hem the other edge of the Collar to the inside of the neckline.

Sleeves

8. Neaten the wrist edges of the Sleeve pieces with zigzag stitches.

9. The Sleeves are put into the Top following the same method as for the T-top on page 23, stage 9 and Fig 4. Match the black dots on the Sleeve, Front and Back patterns.

10. Complete the underarm and side seams as described for the T-top on page 23, stages 10-11 and Fig 5.

Sleeve ends and hem

11. Press the neatened Sleeve ends to the inside to desired length, then machine-stitch 3mm *(⅛in)* from the edge.

12. Make a turned-under hem on the bottom edge of the Top (see page 14 for technique).

Fastenings

13. Measure and mark the positions of the six press-on fasteners. The top fastener is 15mm *(⅝in)* from the neck edge and the lowest fastener is 12mm *(½in)* from the bottom edge.

14. Apply the fasteners to the Top's front opening.

Making the bow-tie

15. Fold and stitch the bow-tie strip of fabric, using the method for making straps on page 15. Sew the open end closed with slipstitches.

16. Tie a single knot in the strip (see picture) to make the bow-tie and sew to the neckline just above the first fastener.

Trousers

Make up the Trousers following the instructions for the Play Pants on page 24, stages 1-6. Then proceed as follows:

7. Neaten the waist edge with zigzag stitching.

8. Turn and press a 15mm *(⅝in)* hem to the inside. Press.

9. Machine-stitch to make an elastic casing (see page 12 for technique).

10. Finish the trouser hems (see page 14 for technique).

Fig 3 *Iron the interfacing to the collar*

Fig 4 *Fold the collar, right sides facing, and machine-stitch the ends*

Fig 5 *Machine-stitch right side of collar to right side of neckline*

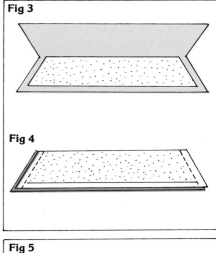

Fig 3

Fig 4

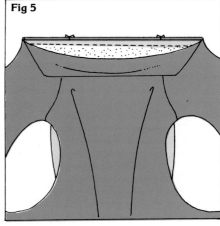

Fig 5

Cuddle suit

This snug two-piece baby suit is made with the T-top pattern on page 22 and the Play Pants pattern on page 24. A few minor alterations to the T-top are necessary to make the faced neckline, and the wrists and trouser legs are elasticated so that the baby is protected from draughts when playing on the floor.

A bought appliqué motif has been applied to the front of the suit (see page 17 for technique).

The adapted pattern would also make a sleeping suit if a soft, brushed cotton fabric were used.

Materials required

To fit sizes chest 48-50cm (19-20in), waist 48-49cm (19-19½in)

Pattern pieces Front 1, Back 2, Sleeve 3, Trousers 4. Cut neck facing from fabric

1.50m *(1⅝yd)* of 91cm *(36in)*-wide fleecy fabric

3m *(3¼yd)* of 12mm *(½in)*-wide elastic

1 button

4cm *(1½in)* of 6mm *(¼in)*-wide ribbon

Matching sewing thread

Alternative fabrics Viyella fabric, poplin, brushed cotton, poly/cotton

Preparation

From the Play Pants graph pattern (Fig 1, page 24), draw a pattern to scale on squared pattern paper.

From the T-top graph pattern (Fig 1, page 22), draw a pattern to scale on squared pattern paper. Follow all instructions for making the patterns and copying in markings.

On the Pants pattern, trim 2cm *(¾in)* from the waist edge.

Following the fabric layout (Fig 1, this page), pin the pattern pieces to the fabric.

Cut out 1 Top Front on the fold of the fabric, cut 2 Top Backs. Cut out 2 Trouser Fronts and 2 Backs. From the remaining fabric, cut a bias strip 36×4cm *(14½×1½in)* for the Top's neck facing.

Making the Top

1. Pin 2 Backs together on the Centre Back seam from the bottom edge to 7.5cm *(3in)* from neck edge. Baste, then machine-stitch the seam. Neaten the edges.
2. On the machine-stitched seam neaten the edges, then fold and baste them to the wrong side for a Back neck opening.
3. Pin Front to Back on the shoulder seams. Baste, machine-stitch and then neaten the edges.

Neck facing

4. Fold and baste a 1cm *(⅜in)* turning on both short ends of the bias strip.
5. Pin and baste one long edge of the strip to the neckline, right sides of fabric together, with the turned ends at Back neck. Machine-stitch the seam (Fig 2).
6. Trim the seam allowance back to 6mm *(¼in)* and clip into the curves to ease the seam.
7. Make a button loop (see page 13 for technique), and baste across the

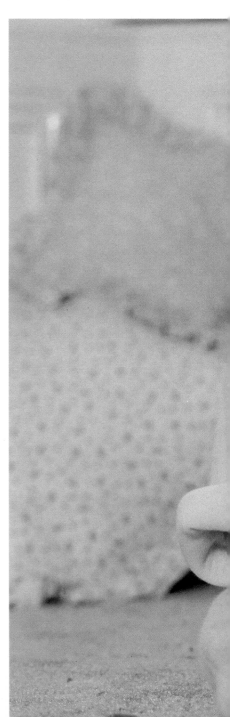

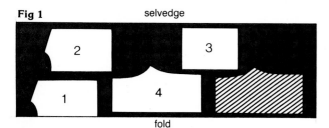

Fig 1 selvedge

fold

Fig 1 *Fabric layout for the Cuddle Suit*

Fig 2 *Apply the bias strip to the neck edge*

Fig 3 *Slipstitch the bias strip on the wrong side*

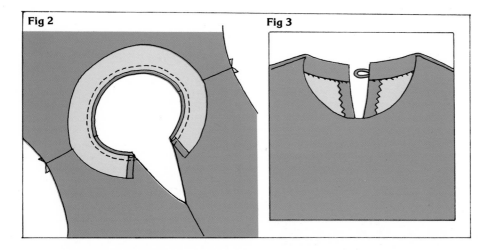

Fig 2   Fig 3

seam allowance, 6mm *(¼in)* down from the neck edge.

8. Turn the facing to the inside of the neckline, turn the raw edge under and hem or slipstitch in place (Fig 3). Slipstitch the ends of the facing at Back neck.

9. Sew a button to correspond with the button loop.

Sleeves

10. Open the Top right side out and lay it flat. Pin the Sleeves to the Top along the armhole edges, right sides of fabric facing and matching black dots. Baste and machine-stitch. Neaten the seam edges.

Underarm and side seams

11. Turn the garment inside out and pin and baste the underarm and side seams. Machine-stitch in one operation, from the bottom edge to the sleeve edges.

12. Clip into the underarm curve for ease. Neaten the seam edges.

Elasticated wrists

13. Turn a 2cm *(¾in)* hem on the Sleeve ends for elastic casings. Zigzag-stitch and insert elastic (see page 12 for technique).

Making the Trousers

14. Follow the instructions on page 24, stages 1-5, for making the Play Pants.

15. Make casings for elastic at the waist edge and the ankles (see page 12 for technique).

All-in-one

One-piece suits are ideal for babies at crawling stage. This suit is back-opening with neck ties.

The square collar, trimmed with novelty heart-shaped buttons, is stitched to a round neckline but the collar could be made to be detachable.

Detachable collars are useful if they become soiled with food and baby needs a quick freshening-up.

Materials required

To fit sizes chest 48-50cm (19-20in), shoulder to ankle 60-62.5cm (24-25in)
Pattern pieces Main piece 1, Collar 2
1m *(1⅛yd)* of 91cm *(36in)*-wide poly/cotton fabric
20×35cm *(8×14in)* piece of white cotton fabric
1m *(1⅛yd)* of 2cm *(¾in)*-wide white bias binding
2 novelty buttons
Matching sewing thread
Alternative fabrics Poplin, brushed cotton, needlecord

Preparation

Fig 1 is the graph pattern for the All-in-One, both Front and Back pieces, and for the Collar. The scale is 1 square=5cm *(2in)* and two sizes are given on the pattern, the smaller size indicated in a coloured line. A seam allowance of 1cm *(⅜in)* has been included on the pattern pieces.

Draw the pattern to scale on squared pattern paper. Cut out the pieces, copying in all markings.

Pin the main pattern piece to the fabric as shown in the fabric layout (Fig 2). Cut out 2 Fronts. Transfer all markings. Unpin the pattern and re-pin to fabric (Fig 2). Cut out 2 Backs. Transfer all markings.

From folded white fabric, cut the Collar, noting that Centre Front is placed to the fold of fabric.

Making the All-in-One

1. Pin 2 Fronts together along the Centre Front seam (A–C on the pattern), right sides of fabric facing. Baste the seam, then machine-stitch.
2. Clip into the curve to ease the seam allowance. Press the seam open. Neaten the seam allowance edges.

3. Pin and baste 2 Back pieces together on the Centre Back seam (from B–C on the pattern). Machine-stitch, then clip into the curved seam. Press the seam open and neaten edges.
4. The open seam on the Back from A–B is the neck opening. Press the seam allowances of the opening to the wrong side and trim the edges with pinking shears. Machine-stitch along the fold edges of the opening.

Joining Front to Back

5. With right sides of fabric facing, pin Front to Back along the shoulder seams. Baste, then machine-stitch.
6. Press the seams open and neaten the edges.

Legs

7. With right sides of fabric facing, pin, baste and then machine-stitch the inside leg seams in one operation. Clip into the curve to ease the seam. Press the seam open and neaten the edges.

Armholes

8. Finish the edges of the armholes with bias binding (see page 11 for applying bias strips).

Collar

9. Turn and press a single narrow hem to the wrong side on all three straight edges of the Collar piece. Machine-stitch 3mm *(⅛in)* from the edge.
10. Placing the right side of the Collar to the wrong side of the neckline, and matching Centre Fronts, pin the Collar to the neckline, setting the pins vertically. The ends of the Collar will lie just beyond the shoulder seams on the neckline edge.
11. Baste, and then machine-stitch

Fig 1 *Graph pattern for the All-in-One and Collar, 1sq=5cm (2in)*

Fig 2 *Fabric layouts for the All-in-One pieces and for the Collar piece*

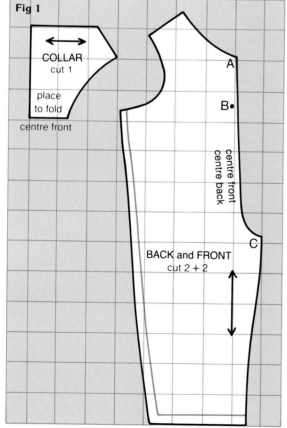

Fig 1

COLLAR
cut 1

place to fold

centre front

A

B•

centre front
centre back

C

BACK and FRONT
cut 2 + 2

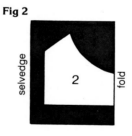

Fig 2

selvedge

2

fold

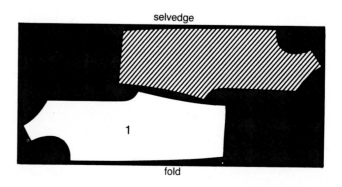

selvedge

1

fold

the Collar in place. Trim the seam allowance back to 3mm *(⅛in)* and oversew the edges. Sew the buttons on the Collar (see picture).

Back neck and ties
12. Cut two pieces of bias binding 30cm *(12in)* long. Bind the back neckline from the ends of the Collar to the Back opening. Machine-stitch the hanging ends of bias binding to make ties (Fig 3; see also page 11 for applying bias strips).

Leg hems
13. Try the suit on the baby to check a comfortable leg length. Turn a narrow hem to the right side, then turn and press a second, 2.5cm *(1in)* hem to the right side. Machine-stitch 3mm *(⅛in)* from the edge of the fold.

Detachable collar
If the collar is to be detachable, work stage 9, then bind the curved edge of the collar with bias binding. Sew the ball part of seven press-studs to the bias binding, spacing them equidistantly.

On the Top neckline bind the edges with bias binding, allowing enough binding to make two back neck ties. Sew the socket part of the press-studs along the neckline to correspond with the collar.

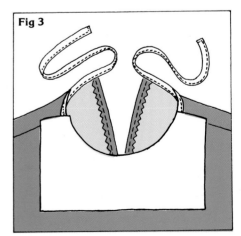

Fig 3 *Finish the back neckline from the ends of the Collar to the Back opening. Machine-stitch the ends of bias binding to make ties*

Toddler Wardrobe

Toddlers, children aged from 1½-3 years, lead active lives and their clothes need to have ease of movement and be comfortable to wear. At the same time, toddlers are just beginning to be interested in their appearance so the patterns in this chapter are exciting and fashionable, which will appeal to this age-group. Some of the patterns are very versatile and, with a change of fabric and minor adaptations, more designs can be achieved.

Pinafore dress

This charming pinafore can be worn over a blouse for a country milkmaid look, or can be worn alone as a sun-dress. The yoke is 'quilted' but can be left plain if preferred.

Materials required

To fit sizes chest 53-56cm (21-22in), shoulder to hem (adjustable) 56-58cm (22-23in)

Pattern pieces Yoke 1. Cut 2 pieces for the Skirt

1.40m *(1½yd)* of 120cm *(48in)*-wide brushed cotton fabric

2m *(2¼yd)* of 1cm *(⅜in)*-wide lace edging

4 pearl press-on fasteners

Matching sewing threads

Alternative fabrics Cotton, cotton mixtures, fine lawn, batiste, seersucker. (All-over cotton lace if the quilting effect is omitted.)

Preparation

Fig 1 is the graph pattern for the Pinafore Dress Yoke. The scale is 1 square=5cm *(2in)* and two sizes are given, the smaller size indicated in a coloured line. A seam allowance of 1cm *(⅜in)* is included on the pattern.

Draw the Yoke pattern on squared pattern paper. Cut out, copying in all markings. The skirt is cut as 2 straight pieces, each 50×97cm *(20×38in)*.

Cut the 2 Skirt pieces across the width of the fabric. Cut the 4 Yoke pieces across the width of fabric. From the remaining fabric, cut two 3.5cm *(1¼in)*-wide strips on the bias, 35cm *(14in)* long, for binding the neckline and straps.

Making the Dress

1. Pin 2 Yoke pieces together, wrong sides of fabric facing. Pin the remaining 2 pieces in the same way.
2. Work basting stitches round the edges of both Yokes.
3. The Yokes are machine-stitched to give a quilted look. Following the guide-lines on the Yoke pattern (Fig 1), and using a ruler and tailors' chalk, draw lines diagonally across both Yoke pieces, 2.5cm *(1in)* apart, to make a diamond pattern.
4. Set the sewing-machine to a medium-length stitch and stitch along the marked lines, first one way, left to right, then the crossing lines, right to left.
5. Bind the shoulder edges and the neckline of the Yokes with bias-cut strips (see page 11 for applying bias strips).
6. Turn in the lower, open edges of the Yokes 6mm *(¼in)* and sew with slipstitches to close. Press the seam.

Skirt

The waist edge of the Skirt pieces is gathered on to the Yokes.

7. Referring to the gathering techniques on page 10, gather both Skirt pieces and then attach the Skirt pieces to the Yokes. Neaten seam edges with zigzag stitches (see page 10 for working gathered fabric).

Side seams

8. Pin, baste and machine-stitch the Skirt side seams, working from a point 5cm *(2in)* below the bottom edges of the Yoke, to the hem. Press open and neaten seam edges.
9. Trim the edges of the armholes and the side Skirt opening with pinking shears. Turn a 1cm *(⅜in)* hem on the edges to the inside of the garment and machine-stitch 3mm *(⅛in)* from the edge (Fig 2).

Hem and fasteners

10. Finish the dress hem following the turned-under hem technique on page 14. Slipstitch lace edging to the fold of the hem.
11. Apply two press-on fasteners to each of the shoulders (see picture).

Party pretty

Make the Pinafore Dress pattern in all-over cotton lace to wear over a dark-coloured dress for a pretty, party look. Omit the yoke stitching.

Sew lace to the tops of ankle socks for a co-ordinated look.

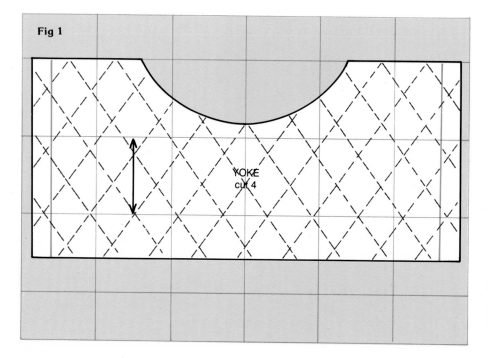

Fig 1

YOKE
cut 4

Fig 1 Graph pattern for the Pinafore Dress Yoke, 1sq=5cm (2in)

Fig 2 The dress, from the wrong side, the armhole and skirt edges pinked and stitched

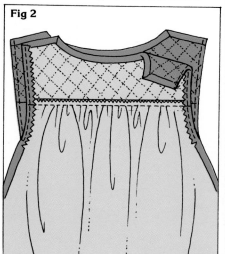

Fig 2

Overshirt

This front-fastening shirt can be worn alone in summer and over a lightweight sweater for winter wear.

The sleeves are cut all in one with the garment for easy sewing, and the collar is a simple bias strip.

The pattern is suitable for both boys and girls. It would make a pretty blouse worn with the fastenings at the back and teamed with a skirt.

Materials required

To fit sizes chest 53-56cm (21-22in), shoulder to hem (adjustable) 28cm (11in)
Pattern pieces Front 1, Back 2. Cut bias strip for Collar
91cm *(36in)* of 91cm *(36in)*-wide Viyella fabric
6 press-on fasteners
Matching sewing thread
Alternative fabrics Seersucker, poplin, viscose fabrics

Preparation

Fig 1 is the graph pattern for the Overshirt. The scale is 1 square=5cm *(2in)* and two sizes are given on the pattern, the smaller size indicated in a coloured line. A seam allowance of 1cm *(⅜in)* is included on the pattern pieces.

Draw the pattern to scale on squared pattern paper. Cut out the pieces, copying in all markings.

Following the fabric layout (Fig 2), pin the pattern pieces to the fabric. Cut out 2 Fronts and 1 Back on the fold. Transfer all markings to fabric.

From remaining fabric, cut a bias strip 48×5cm *(19×2in)* for the Collar.

Making the Shirt

1. Pin Fronts to Back on the shoulder seams, right sides of fabric facing and matching B−B (on the pattern). Baste, then machine-stitch.
2. Press seams open, then neaten the edges.

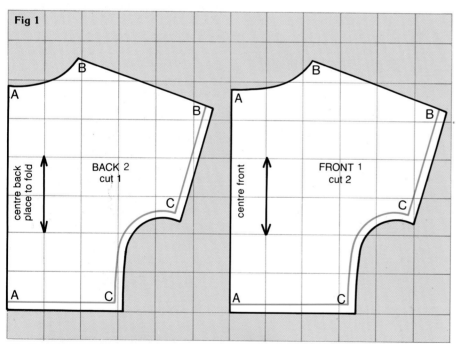

Fig 1

BACK 2
cut 1

centre back
place to fold

FRONT 1
cut 2

centre front

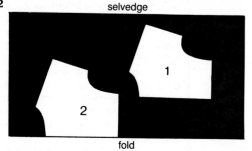

Fig 2

selvedge

fold

Fig 1 *Graph pattern for the Overshirt, 1sq = 5cm (2in)*

Fig 2 *Fabric layout for the Overshirt. The Back is cut on the fold of fabric*

3. On the Front pieces, neaten the Centre Front edges (A–A on the pattern) with zigzag stitching.

4. Measure and chalk-mark a fold line 12mm (½in) from the neatened edges on both Front pieces. Turn the edge to the inside of the garment on the fold line and press.

5. Topstitch 6mm (¼in) from the folded edge.

Collar

6. Fold the bias strip in half lengthwise and, right sides of fabric facing, bind the neck edge of the Shirt (see page 11 for applying bias strips).

7. Turn in the ends of the binding at the front neck edges and hand-sew to neaten.

Underarm and side seams

8. Pin Front to Back along the underarm and side seams (C–C on the pattern). Baste, then machine-stitch. Clip into the curved seam allowance to ease the seam. Press open the seam and neaten the edges.

Sleeve edges and hems

9. Trim the sleeve edges with pinking shears. Turn a hem to the inside to the desired length and stitch 6mm (¼in) from the edge. Press.

10. Pink the bottom edge of the Shirt and turn a hem to the inside of the garment. Machine-stitch 6mm (¼in) from the edge and press.

11. Apply the press-on fasteners to the Shirt's front edges, the top fastener on the collar and the lowest fastener 4.5cm (1¾in) from the hem. Space the remaining fasteners in between.

Edge-to-edge jacket

Omitting the fasteners, the Overshirt makes an attractive edge-to-edge jacket. Make it in a bright cotton print for summer or, perhaps, in velvet for a little girl to wear over a party dress.

Tip When pinning pattern pieces to velvet or corduroy, arrange pieces so that the pile runs the same way on each. Brush your hand over the fabric to decide whether you want the pile to run upwards or downwards – running upwards appears to give greater depth to the colour.

Splash suit

This all-in-one suit is designed to be worn for those messy activities toddlers delight in — helping to wash the car, making mud pies in the garden or enjoying the sand-pit in the rain! Made of machine-washable nylon ciré, the garment is shower-proof and could also be worn as a protective cover-all in wet weather.

Materials required

To fit sizes chest 66-68cm (26-27in), sleeve length 24-25cm (9½-10in), inside leg length (adjustable) 31-34cm (12½-13½in)
Pattern pieces Main pattern piece 1, Sleeve 2
1.50m (1⅝yd) of 120cm (48in)-wide nylon ciré
1 press-on fastener
Matching sewing thread

Preparation

Fig 1 is the graph pattern for the Splash Suit Front and Back piece. The scale is 1 square=5cm (2in) and two sizes are given on the pattern, the smaller size indicated in a coloured line. A seam allowance of 1cm (⅜in) is included on the pattern.

Draw the pattern to scale on squared paper. Cut out the pattern piece, copying in all markings.

Following the fabric layout (Fig 2), pin the pattern to fabric and cut out 2 Fronts. Transfer all markings to fabric, unpin the pattern, re-pin to the fabric (Fig 2) and cut out 2 Backs. Transfer all markings.

Making the Suit

1. Pin 2 Fronts together, right sides of fabric facing, on the Centre Front seam (A–A on the pattern).
2. Baste, then machine-stitch. Trim the seam allowances with pinking shears. (Ciré does not fray so no neatening is required.)
3. Pin 2 Backs together, right sides of fabric facing, from the crotch (A) to the black dot (see pattern). Baste and then machine-stitch the seam. Pink the seam allowance edges.
4. Turn the seam allowance on the Back opening to the inside and machine-stitch 6mm (¼in) from the edge, stitching across the bottom of the opening for a neat look (Fig 3).

Joining Front to Back

5. Pin Front to Back on the shoulder seams (B–B on the pattern). Baste, then machine-stitch. Neaten seam allowances with pinking shears.

Neck edge

6. Trim the neck edge with pinking shears, turn a narrow hem to the inside of the garment, baste, then machine-stitch.

Sleeves

7. With right sides of fabric facing, pin, then baste the Sleeve pieces to the armhole edges, matching C–B–C (see pattern). Machine-stitch and neaten seam edges with pinking shears.

Legs

8. Pin Front and Back together on the inside leg seam (A–D on the pattern). Baste, then machine-stitch in one operation, from leg hem through the crotch and down to the other leg hem. Neaten seam edges with pinking.
9. Pin and baste the side seams and underarm seams together, right sides of fabric facing, then baste.

Machine-stitch in one operation from leg hem through the underarm to the sleeve edge.
10. Trim the sleeve ends and leg hems with pinking shears.

Roll the hems to the outside of the garment to the desired length — no further stitching or neatening is necessary.
11. Apply the press-on fastener to the Back neck.

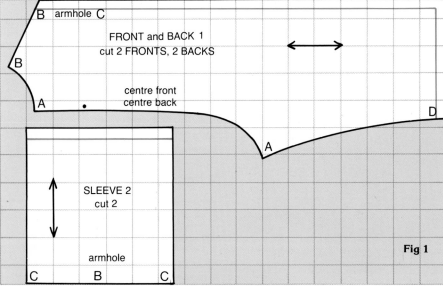

Fig 1 *Graph pattern for the Splash Suit, 1sq = 5cm (2in)*

Fig 2 *Fabric layout for the Splash Suit. The pattern for the main piece is used twice*

Fig 3 *Machine-stitch the Back opening 6mm (¼in) from the edge*

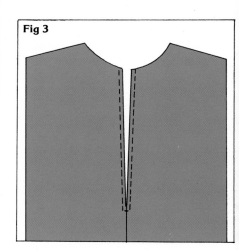

Pyjama suit

This all-in-one suit is made with the
Splash Suit pattern on page 38.

Materials required

*To fit sizes chest 66-68cm (26-27in),
sleeve length 24-25cm (9½-10in),
inside leg length 31-34cm
(12½-13½in)*

Pattern pieces Main pattern piece 1,
    Sleeve 2 (from Fig 1, page 38). Cut
    Collar from fabric

1.50m *(1⅝yd)* of 120cm *(48in)*-wide
    printed cotton fabric

3m *(3¼yd)* of 3cm *(1¼in)*-wide bias
    binding

Matching sewing thread

Alternative fabrics Seersucker,
poplin, brushed cotton, needlecord,
woollen fabrics

Preparation

Follow the instructions on page 38
for drawing the graph pattern and
cutting out the pattern pieces. Use
the fabric layout (Fig 2, page 38) for
cutting out the Pyjama Suit.

    From remaining fabric cut a strip
for the Collar, 80×10cm *(31×4in)*.

Making the Suit

1. Pin 2 Fronts together, right sides
of fabric facing, on the Centre Front
seam (A–A on the pattern). Baste,
then machine-stitch. Press open the
seam and neaten the edges.

2. Pin 2 Backs together, right sides
of fabric facing, from the crotch (A)
to a point 31cm *(12½in)* from neck
edge. Baste, then machine-stitch the
seam. Press the seam open and
neaten the edges.

3. For the Back neck opening, turn a
doubled narrow hem on the raw
edges above the black dot. Press and
machine-stitch.

4. Join Front to Back on the
shoulder seams (B–B on the
pattern). Join inside leg seams. Stitch
in sleeves, using same method as for
Splash Suit, stage 7, on page 38. Pin,
baste, then machine-stitch. Press
seams open and neaten the edges.

Collar

5. Turn and pin a narrow, doubled
hem to the wrong side on one long
edge and the two short ends of the
Collar strip. Baste, then machine-
stitch the hems.

6. Gather the other long edge (see page 10 for technique). Following the technique for working gathered fabric (page 10), stitch the gathered Collar piece to the Suit, right side of Suit to the wrong side of the Collar. Trim the seam allowance back to 6mm *(¼in)*.

7. Cut a strip of bias binding 38cm *(15in)* long. Bind the neck edge of the Suit and frilled Collar (see page 11 for applying bias strips).

Neaten the ends of the binding with hand-sewing.

Ties

8. Cut eight strips of bias binding, each 30cm *(12in)* long.

9. Fold lengthwise and machine-stitch the edges to make ties. At the end, fold under 12mm *(½in)* and hand-sew the fold to the Back neck opening, the top pair to the neckline binding, the remaining three pairs positioned equidistantly down the Back opening. Neaten the ends of the strips with hand-sewing.

Hems

10. Make a turned-under hem on the Suit legs (see page 14 for technique).

Clown pyjama bag

Left-over lengths of fabric can be used to make all kinds of small toys and accessories for children.

A clown pyjama bag is a popular idea for children of any age.

1. Cut 2 pieces of washable fabric 50cm *(20in)* deep by 35cm *(14in)* wide.

2. Slash one piece down the length.

3. Sew the slashed pieces together again, working from the bottom to within 15cm *(6in)* of the top edge. Press and stitch the seam allowances of the opening.

4. Pin, baste and sew the two pieces together on all four sides. Turn to the right side.

5. Stuff the top end with old socks or tights. Tie around the stuffing with tape or ribbon to make a round head.

6. Work a face in embroidery threads or simply sew on buttons for features. Use scraps of knitting wool for hair, or plait strips of scrap fabrics for plaits.

7. Make a frill for the neck, if desired, from scrap fabric or lace.

8. Sew a ribbon or tape loop to the back of the head.

Tough denims

The Jeans and Jacket, made of cotton denim, are an ideal outfit for active toddlers. The Jeans are calf-length so that they are comfortable to wear with boots or wellingtons. The Jacket has a zipped front opening and a tie waist. The garments can, of course, be worn separately, the Jeans teaming with shirts and sweaters, and the Jacket with trousers.

Materials required

To fit sizes chest 53-56cm (21-22in), waist 50-52cm (20-20½in), inside leg 24cm (9½in)

Pattern pieces Jacket Front 1, Back 2, Sleeve 3, Jeans Front 4, Belt Loop 5. Cut Tie Belts, Loops and Collar from fabric
1.20m (1⅜yd) of 91cm (36in)-wide cotton denim for Jacket
1.10m (1¼yd) of 91cm (36in)-wide cotton denim for Jeans
25cm (10in)-long open-ended heavyweight zip fastener for Jacket
8 press-on fasteners
Matching and contrasting sewing threads

Alternative fabrics Cotton, poly/cotton, needlecord, corduroy, linen-type fabrics and viscose fabrics

Preparation

Fig 1 is the graph pattern for the Jeans and Jacket pieces and the scale is 1 square=5cm (2in). Two sizes are given on the pattern, the smaller size indicated in a coloured line. A seam allowance of 1cm (⅜in) is included on the pattern.

Draw the pattern pieces to scale on squared pattern paper. Cut out the pieces, copying in all markings. Following the fabric layout (Fig 2), pin the pattern pieces to fabric.

Cut out 2 Fronts, 1 Back and 2 Sleeves for the Jacket. Cut 2 Fronts, 2 Backs and 8 Belt Loops for the Jeans.

From the remaining fabric, cut 1 Tie Belt 113×3cm (44×1¼in) and 1 Collar piece on the bias of fabric 43×8cm (17×3¼in). Cut 4 Belt Loops each 5×3cm (2×1¼in) for the Jacket.

Cut a belt 64×6cm (25×2½in) for the Jeans.

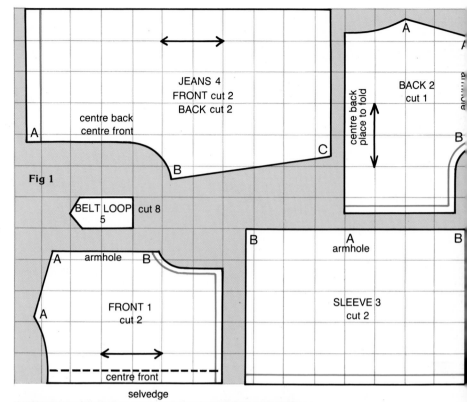

Fig 1 *Graph pattern for the Tough Denims, 1sq=5cm (2in)*

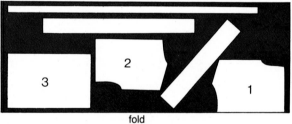

Fig 2 *Fabric layouts for the Denim Jacket and Jeans*

Making the Jacket

1. Fold and press the Centre Front edges to the wrong side on the facing lines (on the pattern). Neaten the edges with pinking shears.
2. Insert the zip fastener between the Front edges (see page 13 for technique). Position the zip 15mm (⅝in) from the neck edge and the bottom edge. Use the contrasting thread to machine-stitch the zip in position.
3. Join the Front to the Back on the shoulder seams (A−A on pattern).

Baste, then machine-stitch. Press the seam open and neaten the edges.

Collar

4. Fold the Collar strip in half lengthwise. Pin. Using tailors' chalk (and a coin if it helps), draw a curve on the ends. Stitch along the chalked lines (Fig 3, page 44).
5. Trim off the surplus seam allowance to 3mm (⅛in). Turn the Collar right side out and press.
6. Pin the Collar to the neckline, right sides of fabric facing, starting at

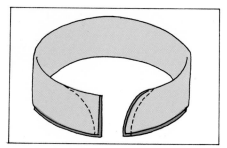
Fig 3 Draw a curve at the ends, machine-stitch and trim back the seam allowance

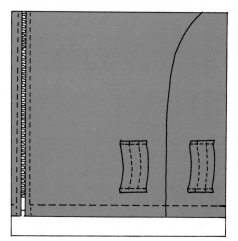
Fig 4 Machine-stitch the Jacket Belt Loops each side of the side seams

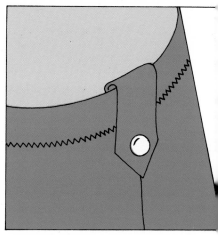
Fig 5 Jeans Belt Loops are stitched to the inside of the waistband, over the seams

the Front neck edges. Baste and machine-stitch. Trim the seam allowances to 6mm (¼in).
7. Turn a hem on the other edge of the Collar and slipstitch to the inside of the neckline.

Sleeves
8. With right sides of fabric facing, pin the Sleeves to the Jacket on the armhole edges, matching points B−A−B (on the pattern). Baste and then machine-stitch. Press the seams open and neaten the edges.

Underarm and side seams
9. Pin Front to Back on the underarm and side seams, right sides of fabric facing. Baste and then machine-stitch in one continuous operation from the bottom edge to the Sleeve ends.
    Clip into the curve for ease, press open the seam and neaten the edges.
10. Make turnings on the Sleeve ends for elastic casings (see page 12 for technique). Insert elastic and close the seam.

Bottom edge
11. Make a narrow, turned-under hem on the bottom edge of the Jacket, the hem level with the bottom of the zip fastener. Machine-stitch the hem with contrasting thread.
12. On each of the 4 Belt Loop pieces, turn a single hem to the wrong side on all edges. Press, then baste. Work two rows of machine-stitching down the length of the loops, 6mm (¼in) from the edges.
13. Pin and baste the Loops to the right side of the Jacket 2cm (¾in) from the side seams, two at the front and two at the Back, and positioned just above the hem line stitching. Machine-stitch across the bottom and top edges of the loops (Fig 4).

Belt
14. Make a Tie Belt for the Jacket (see page 15 for technique). Thread the Belt through the Belt Loops to tie at the front.

Appliqué decoration
15. Cut 4cm (1½in) squares from fabric scraps and press narrow turnings to the wrong side all round. Baste the squares in place on the Jacket Front and machine-stitch

3mm (⅛in) from the edges, working each square individually. (Alternatively, work the appliqué following the technique on page 17, or apply a purchased motif.)

Making the Jeans
1. Pin 2 Fronts together, right sides of fabric facing, on the Centre Front seam (A−B on the pattern).
2. Baste and then machine-stitch the seam. Clip into the curve for ease, then press the seam open. Neaten the edges.
3. Join the 2 Back pieces in the same way.
4. Pin and baste the inside leg seam. Machine-stitch the seam in one operation from leg hem through the crotch to the other leg hem (see page 9 for the technique of reducing bulk in crossed seams).
5. Clip into the curves for ease, press seams open and neaten the edges.
6. Pin Front to Back on side seams. Baste, then machine-stitch. Press seams open and neaten the edges.
7. Turn a hem at the waist edge on the fold line marked on the pattern. Stitch the turning, using zigzag stitching and matching thread.

Belt
8. Make a belt following the technique on page 15. Fit the finished belt on the child and apply two press-on fasteners to fasten the belt at the front.

Belt Loops
9. The Belt Loop pieces are worked in pairs to make 4 Belt Loops. Follow

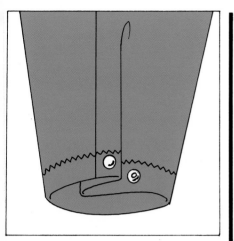

Fig 6 *Apply the top section of the fastener through two thicknesses of fabric to shape legs*

the technique on page 15 for making shaped straps and tabs, but leave the straight, short ends open for turning to the right side. Complete the Loops and turn to the right side. Press.
10. Machine-stitch across the straight ends to close the seam. Pin the Loops to the inside of the waistband, positioning each one over a seam, Centre Front, Centre Back and the side seams. Align the straight edge of the Loops with the zigzag stitching of the waistband. Stitch the Loops in place, working zigzag stitching over the same previous stitching line (Fig 5).
11. Apply press-on fasteners to the shaped end of the Belt Loops and to the Jeans to correspond (see picture).

Leg hems
12. Neaten the leg edges with pinking shears. Turn the hems to the inside of the garment and press. Stitch with zigzag machine-stitch in matching thread.

Shaping legs
13. Make a fold in the fabric 2cm (¾in) from the side seam on both legs. Press the fold. Apply the top section of the press-on fastener, punching through both layers of fabric.
14. Apply the ball section of the fastener 4cm (1½in) from the seam line (Fig 6).

If a conventional leg finish is preferred, cut the Jeans to the desired length at preparation stage and then work a turned-under hem.

Pink and grey
This simple two-piece outfit is made with the Overshirt pattern on page 36 for the Top, and the Jeans pattern on page 42 for the Trousers.

It is an example of the versatility of the wardrobe's designs and the different looks that can be achieved with minor adaptations to patterns and a different choice of fabric.

Materials required
To fit sizes chest 53-56cm (21-22in), waist 50-53cm (20-21in), inside leg 23cm (9in)
66cm *(26in)* of 91cm *(36in)*-wide pink poly/cotton fabric
1.50m *(1⅝yd)* of grey poly/cotton fabric
50cm *(20in)* of 1cm *(⅜in)*-wide elastic
15mm *(⅝in)* button mould (for covering)
Matching sewing threads
Alternative fabrics Seersucker, cotton, viscose fabrics

Preparation
Follow the instructions on page 36 for drawing out the graph pattern and cutting out the pattern pieces for the Overshirt.

The Pink Top has a back neck opening, so to adapt the Overshirt pattern, mark the front pattern piece as Back, and the back pattern piece as Front.

Pin the pattern pieces to the pink fabric (Fig 1, this page), pinning the Front to the fold of fabric. Cut out 1 Front and 2 Backs.

Draw the graph pattern for the Jeans (Fig 1, page 42) and cut out the pattern pieces. Pin to the grey fabric as shown in the fabric layout (Fig 1, this page) and cut out 2 Fronts and 2 Backs.

From the remaining grey fabric, cut two patch pockets each 15×14cm *(6×5½in)*. Cut a bias strip

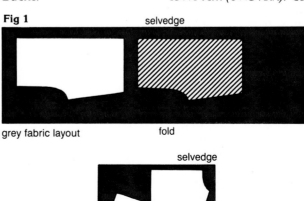

Fig 1

selvedge

grey fabric layout   fold

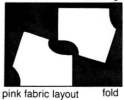

selvedge

pink fabric layout   fold

Fig 1 *Fabric layouts for the pink and grey fabrics*

45×2cm *(18 × ¾in)* for binding the Top's neck edge. Cover the button mould with a scrap of grey fabric.

Making the Top

1. Pin the 2 Backs together, right sides facing, on the Centre Back seam (A – A on the pattern), from the bottom edge to a point 10cm *(4in)* from the neck edge.

Baste, then machine-stitch. Press the seam open and neaten the edges.
2. Pin the Front and Back together, right sides facing, on the shoulder seams. Baste and machine-stitch, then press the seams open and neaten the edges.

Neckline

3. Bind the neck edge with the grey bias strip (see page 11 for applying bias strips). Hand-sew the binding ends at the Back neck to neaten them.
4. Sew the covered button to one side of the neckline and make a fabric button loop (see page 13 for technique). Sew the loop to the opposite side of the neckline.

Pockets

5. Make a 6mm *(¼in)* turning to the wrong side on all four edges of both Pocket pieces. Press and then machine-stitch 3mm *(⅛in)* from the fold for the top edge of the Pockets.
6. Pin and baste the Pockets to the Front, setting them at an angle (see picture), with the bottom corners 4cm *(1½in)* from the bottom edge and 3cm *(1¼in)* from the side seam edges.

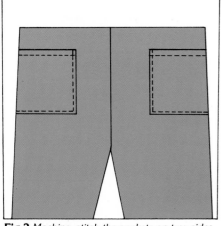

Fig 2 *Machine-stitch the pockets on two sides*

Underarm and side seams

7. Pin and baste Front to Back on the side and underarm seams, from a point 5cm *(2in)* from the bottom edge, to the sleeve edge. (This makes a slit opening on both side seams.)
8. Machine-stitch the seams in one operation. Clip into the curved seam for ease. Press the seams open and neaten the edges.
9. Press the seam allowance on the slit openings to the wrong side of the garment and neaten the edges with pinking shears.

Sleeves

10. Turn a narrow, double hem to the wrong side on the Sleeve ends and machine-stitch.

Hem

11. Make a 6mm *(¼in)* turned-under hem on the bottom edge of the Top. Press.

Making the Trousers

1. Pin 2 Fronts together on the Centre Front seam (A – B on the pattern). Baste, then machine-stitch.
2. Press the seam flat to one side, trim the seam allowance back to 6mm *(¼in)* and neaten the edges with zigzag stitches.
3. Pin 2 Backs together and baste, machine-stitch and finish as for the Fronts.

Trouser Pockets

The Pockets are set into the side seams on one edge.
4. Make a 15mm *(⅝in)* turning on one short edge on both Pocket pieces, press and then machine-stitch. This is the top edge of the Pockets.
5. Make a 6mm *(¼in)* turning on the opposite short edge, press and baste.
6. On the right-hand side Pocket, make a 6mm *(¼in)* turning on the left-hand edge. On the left-hand side pocket, make a 6mm *(¼in)* turning on the right-hand edge. Baste the turnings.
7. Baste the Pockets to the Trousers Back, the top edges 5cm *(2in)* from the waist edge and the raw edges aligned with the edges of the side seams.
8. Machine-stitch on two sides (Fig 2).

Joining Front to Back

9. Pin the Front and Back together on the inside leg seams, right sides facing. Baste and then machine-stitch. Clip into the seam allowance at the crotch to ease the seam. Trim the seam allowance to 6mm *(¼in)* and neaten with zigzag machine-stitches.
10. Pin and baste the side seams, right sides facing, and then machine-stitch, catching in the edges of the pockets as you stitch. Press the seam allowance to one side, trim back to 6mm *(¼in)* and neaten with zigzag stitches.

Waist

11. Make a turning to the inside of the garment on the waist fold line (marked on the pattern). Make a narrow fold on the raw edge and then machine-stitch to make a casing for elastic, leaving a 5cm *(2in)* gap in the seam at Centre Back.
12. Measure and mark a second casing line halfway down from the top edge of the casing and machine-stitch, again leaving the seam open at Centre Back.
13. Insert elastic (see page 12 for technique). Finish the elastic ends as instructed. Close the casings with machine-stitching.
14. Make turned-under hems on the trouser legs (see page 14 for technique).

Country style

A furnishing fabric with a pretty flower pattern has been used to make this charming country style dress. The fabric is hard-wearing and machine-washable, so it is ideal for active little girls.

The skirt is two straight pieces of fabric, gathered on to a high yoke.

Materials required

To fit sizes chest 53-56cm (21-22in), shoulder to hem 58cm (23in), sleeve 25cm (10in)
Pattern pieces Front Yoke 1, Back Yoke 2, Sleeve 3. Cut 2 Skirt pieces from fabric
1.90m (2yd) of 120cm (48in)-wide cotton furnishing fabric
1.40m (1½yd) of 2.5cm (1in)-wide polyester ribbon

Matching sewing thread
Alternative fabrics Cotton, cotton mixtures, needlecord, velvet

Preparation

Fig 1 is the graph pattern for the Yokes and the Sleeve. The scale is 1 square=5cm (2in) and two sizes are given on the pattern, the smaller size indicated in a coloured line. A seam allowance of 1cm (⅜in) is included on the pattern.

Draw the pattern to scale on squared pattern paper. Cut out the pieces, copying in all markings.

Pin the pattern pieces to the fabric. Cut out 2 Front Yokes on the fold of fabric. Cut out 4 Back Yokes. Cut out 2 Sleeves. Transfer all markings to fabric.

From the fabric, cut 2 pieces for the Skirt 50×97cm (20×38in).

Cut one of the pieces down the middle to make 2 pieces measuring 50×48.5cm (20×19in). These pieces will be referred to as 'Backs'.

Making the Dress

1. Pin one Front Yoke piece to 2 Back Yoke pieces, right sides of fabric facing, at the shoulder seams (C–C on the pattern). Baste, then machine-stitch. (The remaining Front Yoke and 2 Back Yoke pieces are for the Yoke Facing and will be referred to in this way.)
2. Pin, baste and machine-stitch on the shoulder seams, right sides of fabric facing.
3. Press open the seam allowances and neaten the edges.
4. Pin the Yoke and Yoke Facing together on the neck edges only (A–B–C on the pattern), right sides of fabric facing.
5. Baste, then machine-stitch (Fig 2).
6. Still with right sides of fabric facing, pin, baste and then machine-stitch the Back opening edges from A to the black dot (see pattern). Clip into the corners of the neckline and trim back all seams to 6mm (¼in) (Fig 3).
7. Turn the Yoke to the right side and press the edges.

Skirt

8. Pin the 2 Back skirt pieces together again along the cut edges, from the hem to a point 14cm (5½in) from the top edge. Baste, then machine-stitch. Press the seam open and neaten.
9. Press the seam allowances on the

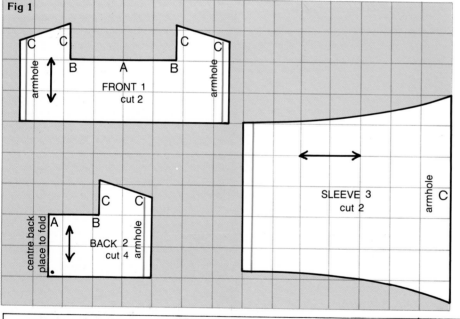

Fig 1 Graph pattern for the Yoke pieces and Sleeve, 1sq=5cm (2in)

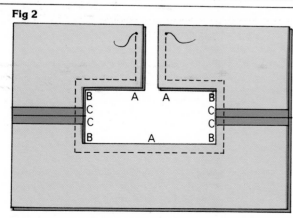

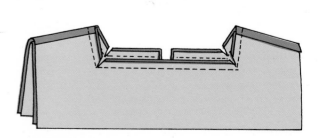

Fig 2 Machine-stitch the neck edge then the Back opening edges

Fig 3 Trim seam allowances and clip into corners

Back waist opening to the wrong
side and trim the edges with pinking
shears.

10. Gather the top edges of both
Skirt pieces, pulling up the gathers
to fit the Skirt pieces to the bottom
edges of the Yoke (see page 10 for
gathering techniques).

   The Skirt pieces are attached to
the Yoke only at this stage, the Yoke
Facing being left unstitched.

11. Pin, then baste the gathered Skirt
pieces to the Front and Back Yoke
(see page 10 for technique). Machine-
stitch, trim the seam allowance back
to 6mm (¼in) and neaten with
zigzag machine-stitching.

Sleeves

12. Lay the garment flat, the right
side facing upwards. Pin the Sleeves
to the Dress on the armhole edges,
right sides of fabric facing. The mark
C on the pattern aligns with the
Dress shoulder seam.

13. Baste and machine-stitch Sleeves
to Dress, stitching through the Yoke
only, leaving the Yoke Facing
unstitched. Finish the Sleeve ends by
turning a hem and machine-
stitching.

Underarm and side seams

14. Pin and baste the side seams and
underarm seams together, right sides
of fabric facing together. Machine-
stitch in one operation. Clip into the
curved seam, press the seam open
and neaten edges.

Yoke Facings

15. Make a 1cm (⅜in) turning to the
wrong side on the Yoke Facing
edges. Hand-sew the Yoke Facing to
the stitching line of Yoke and Skirt,
leaving the armhole edges
unstitched. Work running stitches on
these edges to neaten. Press.

Hem

16. Make a turned-under hem on the
bottom edge to the desired length
(see page 14 for technique).

Finishing

17. Cut the ribbon into four equal
pieces and stitch to the Back neck
opening to make ties, the top tie on
the neck edge and the other tie 5cm
(2in) below.

Pre-School Wardrobe

From around 3 years old, children like to wear bright colours and styles that imitate designs worn by older children. This wardrobe of clothes, designed for 3–5-year-olds, accents colour and fun in such outfits as the tri-coloured top and trousers, smart styling in a black and white striped waistcoat suit, and pretty femininity in a delicate summer cotton dress.

Popper skirt

Most of the clothes in this book are simple enough for a beginner at sewing, but the Popper Skirt is so quick and easy that a little girl might even be able to help to make it herself.

Materials required

To fit sizes waist 53-55cm (21-21½in), length waist to hem (adjustable) 38cm (15in)
Pattern pieces Cut 1 Skirt piece and 2 Straps from fabric
60cm *(24in)* of 120cm *(48in)*-wide cloqué cotton fabric
46cm *(18in)* of 2.5cm *(1in)*-wide bias binding
50cm *(20in)* of 12mm *(½in)*-wide elastic
4 press-on fasteners
Matching sewing thread
Alternative fabrics Cotton prints, woollen fabrics, seersucker, needlecord

Preparation

Cut the Skirt piece 114×43cm *(45×17in)*. Cut 2 Straps 68×9cm *(27×3½in)*.

Making the Skirt

1. Pin the short sides of the Skirt piece together, right sides facing. Baste and machine-stitch. Press the seams open and neaten the edges.
2. Turn a 2cm *(¾in)* hem on the waist edge.
3. Following the technique for applied casings on page 12, make an elastic casing on the waist edge using bias binding. Insert the elastic and finish the elastic casing as described on page 12.
4. Make a turned-under hem on the bottom edge (see page 14 for technique).

Straps

5. Make the straps following the techniques on page 15. Machine-stitch across the ends and then machine-stitch to the inside back waist of the skirt, stitching above the casing, so that the elastic is not caught in the stitching.
6. Apply press-on fasteners to the other end of the straps and to the front inside waist of the skirt. Cross the straps before fastening them.

Tabard

The Tabard is made from two rectangles of fabric held together with press-on fasteners, and has a deep pocket at the front.

Materials required

Finished size 47cm (18½in) wide and 57cm (22½in) long
Pattern pieces Cut 2 pieces for Tabard and 1 Pocket from fabric 90cm *(35½in)* of 120cm *(48in)*-wide cotton fabric
8 press-on fasteners
Matching sewing thread
Alternative fabrics Denim, poplin, sailcloth, plasticised fabrics

Preparation

From the fabric, cut 2 Tabard pieces 50cm *(20in)* wide by 60cm *(24in)* and mark one as Front and the other Back with tailors' chalk.

Cut 1 Pocket piece, so that one long edge is on the selvedge of the fabric 45cm *(18in)* wide and 24cm *(9½in)* deep. Mark chalk lines on the Pocket for pocket divisions (Fig 1).

Making the Tabard

1. Press a 2cm *(¾in)* turning to the wrong side on all four sides of both Tabard pieces.
2. Pin, baste and then stitch, using a wide zigzag stitch.

Pocket

3. Leave the top, selvedge edge of the Pocket piece and press a 1cm *(⅜in)* turning to the wrong side on the other long side and the two short sides.
4. Pin and baste the turnings, then pin the pocket to the Tabard Front, the lower and side edges aligning with the zigzag stitching on the bottom and side edges of the Tabard.
5. Machine-stitch 6mm *(¼in)* from the edges of the pocket.
6. Machine-stitch on the chalked lines to make pocket divisions.
7. Apply three press-on fasteners to the top edges of the Tabard, on the seam allowance, spacing them about 2.5cm *(1in)* apart, to make shoulder fastenings (see picture).
8. Apply a press-on fastener to both sides of the Tabard, positioning them level with the top edge of the pocket, for side fastenings.

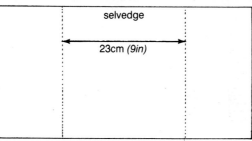

Fig 1 *Measure and mark lines for stitching the pocket divisions*

Tri-coloured suit

This bright summer suit, made in three different colours, is an ideal way of using up remnants of fabric – although, of course, it could also be made in just one, or two, colours. The bound neckline has back ties but a button and button loop could be used if you prefer (see page 13). For a smart, fashion detail, the top has a neat, front pleat.

Materials required

To fit sizes chest 58·60cm (23·24in), waist 53·55cm (21·21½in), inside leg length 44cm (17in)
Pattern pieces Front 1, Back 2, Sleeves 3, Trousers 4. Cut 2 Pockets from fabric

1m *(1⅛yd)* of 120cm *(48in)*·wide white cotton fabric
40cm *(16in)* of 120cm *(48in)*·wide blue cotton fabric
40cm *(16in)* of 120cm *(48in)*·wide yellow cotton fabric
1 packet of 2cm *(¾in)*·wide white cotton bias binding
30cm *(12in)* of 2cm *(¾in)*·wide soft elastic
Matching sewing threads
Alternative fabrics Poplin, seersucker

Preparation

Fig 1 is the graph pattern for the Top and the Trousers. The scale is 1 square=5cm *(2in)* and two sizes are given on the pattern, the smaller size indicated in a coloured line. A seam allowance of 1cm *(⅜in)* is included on the pattern pieces.

Draw the pattern to scale on squared paper. Cut out all the pieces, copying in all markings.

Following the fabric layout (Fig 2), pin the pattern pieces to the fabric. **Top** Cut 1 Front on the fold of the fabric and 2 Backs. Cut 2 Sleeves. **Trousers** Cut 2 Fronts, then unpin and re-pin the pattern to cut 2 Backs, transferring all markings to fabric first.

Transfer all markings on patterns to fabric and unpin the patterns.

Cut two trouser pockets from remaining blue fabric, 22cm *(8½in)* deep and 14cm *(5½in)* wide.

Making the Trousers

1. Pin 2 Fronts together on the Centre Front seam (B–A on the pattern). Baste and then machine-stitch the seam. Clip into the curved seam for ease, then press the seam open and neaten.
2. Make up the 2 Trouser Backs in the same way.
3. Pin, baste and then machine-stitch the inside leg seam (C–B–C on the pattern), stitching in one operation from leg hem through the crotch and down to the other leg hem (see page 9 for the technique of reducing fabric bulk in crossed seams).
Press the seams open, clip into curves and neaten seam edges.

Pockets

4. Turn, press and topstitch a doubled hem on one short edge of both pockets. Work stitching in white thread for contrast. This is the top edge of the pockets.
5. Turn and press a 6mm *(¼in)* hem on the other short side and then on the left-hand edge of one pocket and on the right-hand edge of the other pocket, viewed from the right side.
6. Pin the pockets to the Trouser Front, the top edges lying 4cm *(1½in)* below the fold line of the casing (marked on the pattern). The raw edges of the pockets lie level with the raw edges of the side seams.
7. Baste the pockets in place and then topstitch in white thread 3mm *(⅛in)* from the folded edges, on the inside long edge and the bottom edge. The raw edges at the seams are not stitched at this stage. (An illustration of this method of applying pockets is on page 46.)

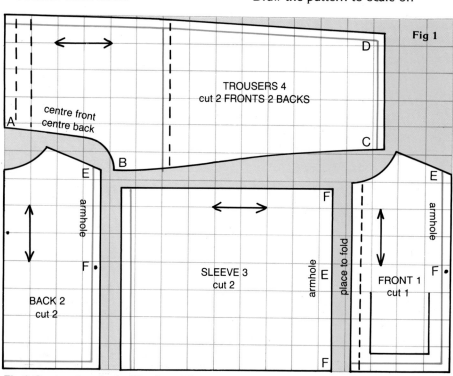

Fig 1 *Graph pattern for the Tri·coloured Suit, 1sq=5cm (2in)*

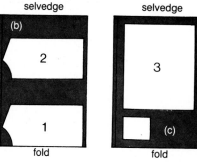

Fig 2 *Fabric layouts for the Tri·coloured Suit: (a) white fabric, (b) yellow fabric, (c) blue fabric*

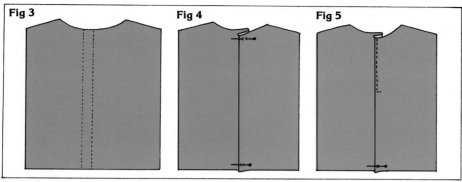

Fig 3 *Making the Front pleat: mark a pleat line 2cm (¾in) from the Centre Front line*

Fig 4 *Fold the pleat line to the Centre Front line and pin*

Fig 5 *Machine-stitch from the neckline, making a right-angled turn*

Side seams

8. Pin, baste and then machine-stitch the side seams, right sides facing and catching in the edges of the pockets. Press seams open and neaten edges.

Elastic casing

9. Turn a hem to the wrong side at the waist edge, on the fold line marked on the pattern. Complete the elastic casing and insert the elastic (see page 12 for technique).

Hems

10. Work a turned-under hem on both Trouser legs, C-D on pattern (see page 14 for technique).

Making the Top

1. Pin 2 Backs together on the Centre Back seam, from the bottom edge to the black dot marking (see pattern).
2. Baste and machine-stitch the seam. Press the seam open and neaten the edges.
3. Above the black dot, press the seam allowance to the wrong side for a Back neck opening. Neaten the seam allowance with pinking shears and then topstitch 3mm (⅛in) from the fold.
4. Mark the Centre Front line on the Front piece with tailors' chalk. Measure and mark a second, parallel line to the right 2cm (¾in) away (Fig 3). This is the pleat line.
5. Working on the ironing board, and with the fabric right side up, bring the pleat line over to meet the Centre Front line. Press firmly. Pin the pleat temporarily at the neck edge and at the hem (Fig 4).
6. Measuring from the neck edge,

chalk a mark 14cm (5½in) down the pleat. Topstitch, using matching thread, from the neck edge to this mark, 3mm (⅛in) from the fold. When the mark is reached, make a right-angled turn as follows: leave the needle in the work, lift the presser foot, turn the work at right angles and then continue stitching for 15mm (⅝in) across the pleat (Fig 5). Remove pins.

Joining Front to Back

7. Pin Front to Back on the shoulder seams, right sides of fabric facing. Baste and machine-stitch. Press seams open and neaten the edges.

Neckline

8. Cut a piece of bias binding to fit round the neckline plus 30cm (12in). Mark the centre of the binding and match this to Centre Front.
9. Following the technique on page 11 for applying bias strips, bind the neckline leaving the ends free at the back for ties.
10. Fold the binding ends and machine-stitch for ties, neatening the ends with hand-sewing.

Sleeves

11. Open the Top out and lay it flat, right sides facing upwards. Pin the Sleeve pieces, right sides to right sides of fabric, along the armhole edge, matching marks F-E-F (see pattern). The technique for attaching sleeves in this way is illustrated on page 23, Fig 4.
12. Baste, then machine-stitch the sleeves to the garment. Press open the seams and neaten the edges.

Side seams

13. The side seams have a slit opening at the hem. Working from the black dot marking (see pattern), pin and baste the side seams, then the underarm seams, together.
14. Machine-stitch from the slit opening to the sleeve edges in one operation. Clip into the curves for ease, then press seams open and neaten edges.

Hem

15. Open the pleat at the hem and make a turned-under hem. Machine-stitch and then re-press the pleat.
16. On the sleeve ends, turn a narrow hem to the inside and press. Turn a second, 2cm (¾in), hem. Press and topstitch. Roll sleeves to length desired.

Waistcoat suit

This smart outfit is made from the versatile Tri-coloured Suit pattern on page 54 and is an indication of the many variations that can be achieved with one pattern, a few minor adaptations and a different fabric.

Materials required

To fit sizes chest 58-60cm (23-24in), waist 53-55cm (21-21½in), inside leg length 45cm (18in)
Pattern pieces From the pattern (Fig 1, page 54) Front 1, Back 2, Trousers 3 (see Preparation of pattern)
2m (2¼yd) of 120cm (48in)-wide printed cotton fabric
30cm (12in) of 2cm (¾in)-wide elastic
Matching sewing threads
Alternative fabrics Poplin, needlecord, denim, lightweight woollen fabric

Preparation

Following the graph pattern (Fig 1, page 54), draw and cut out the pattern pieces for the Trousers and the Top, omitting the Sleeve piece.

Re-mark the Front pattern as Waistcoat Back. Re-mark the Back pattern as Waistcoat Front.

Following the fabric layout (Fig 1, opposite), pin the pattern pieces to the fabric. Cut out 2 Trouser Fronts and 2 Trouser Backs.

Cut out 2 Waistcoat Backs on the fold of fabric. Cut out 4 Waistcoat Fronts. Cut 1 Pocket piece 10cm *(4in)* square from remaining fabric. Transfer all markings to fabric.

Making the Waistcoat
1. The Pocket is worked first. Turn and press a 1cm *(⅜in)* turning on one edge of the Pocket piece. Topstitch 6mm *(¼in)* from the edge. This is the top edge of the pocket.
2. Turn and press a 1cm *(⅜in)* turning on the bottom edge and the left-hand edge of the pocket (viewed from the right side). Baste.
3. Pin and baste the pocket to the right side of 1 Front piece (Fig 2), aligning the raw edge of the pocket with the raw edge of the side seam and 2.5cm *(1in)* from the bottom edge.
4. Machine-stitch, working two rows of machine-stitching about 3mm *(⅛in)* apart.

Joining Fronts to Backs
5. Pin 2 Front pieces (one with the pocket), to a Back piece, on the shoulder seams and right sides of fabric facing. Baste and machine-stitch. Press seams open and neaten the edges.
6. Pin, baste and machine-stitch the side seam from the hem to the underarm (marked with a dot on the pattern). Press the seam open and neaten edges.
7. The remaining Back piece and 2 Front pieces are the Waistcoat lining. Make up the lining in the same way as for the Waistcoat, stages 5 and 6, omitting references to the pocket.
8. With right sides of fabric facing, pin the Waistcoat and the lining together round the neckline and down the Front edges. Baste. Machine-stitch. Trim the seam

allowances back to 3mm *(⅛in)* to reduce bulk. Clip into the curved seams to ease (Fig 3).
9. Turn the garment to the right side and press.
10. Make 6mm *(¼in)* turnings to the inside of the garment on the armhole edges. Press and baste the edges together. Machine-stitch close to the edge.

Hem
11. Fold a 6mm *(¼in)* turning to the inside on the Waistcoat and lining hems. Press and baste the edges together. Machine-stitch close to the edge.

Making the Trousers
Follow the instructions for making the Trousers, stages 1-3 and 8-10, for the Tri-coloured Suit on pages 54-56.

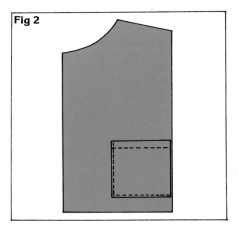

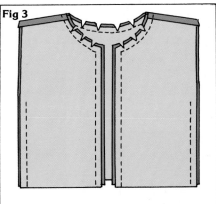

Fig 1 *Fabric layout for the Waistcoat Suit*

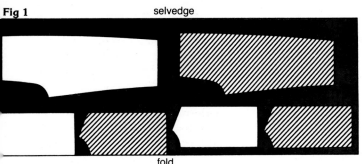

Fig 2 *Baste the prepared pocket to the right side of the left Front*

Fig 3 *Machine-stitch round the neckline and down the Fronts of the Waistcoat and lining, right sides facing*

Sun set

This top and shorts set is ideal for playing in the garden – or on the beach – on hot days. For coolness, the top has an open back, tying at the neck, and the shorts are elastic-waisted for comfort.

It is a design that both girls and boys can wear. The pattern is an adaptation of the Tri-coloured Suit on page 54.

Materials required

To fit sizes chest 58-60cm (23-24in), waist 53-55cm (21-21½in)
Pattern pieces Front 1, Back 2, Shorts 3
40cm *(16in)* of 120cm *(48in)*-wide printed cotton fabric
40cm *(16in)* of 120cm *(48in)*-wide white cotton fabric
1m *(1⅛yd)* of 3cm *(1¼in)*-wide bias binding
30cm *(12in)* of 6mm *(¼in)*-wide elastic
Matching sewing thread
Alternative fabrics Seersucker, lightweight denim, poplin, poly/cotton

Preparation

Working from the graph pattern (Fig 1, page 54), draw and cut out the Trousers pattern, working to the broken lines (on pattern) for the waistline and leg length of the Shorts.

From the same graph pattern, draw and cut out the pattern pieces for the Top's Front and Back, omitting the Sleeve piece.

Following the fabric layout (Fig 1, this page), pin the pattern pieces to fabrics. Cut out 1 Front on the fold from printed fabric, and 2 Backs on the selvedges.

From the white fabric, cut out 2 Shorts Fronts and 2 Backs. (No pocket pieces are required.)

Making the Shorts

1. Pin 2 Fronts together, right sides facing, on the Centre Front seam. Baste and then machine-stitch. Press seams open and neaten the edges.
2. Work the 2 Back pieces in the same way.
3. Pin, baste and machine-stitch the inside leg seam, right sides facing. Clip the curve for ease. Press seams open and neaten the edges.
4. Pin, baste and machine-stitch Front to Back on the side seams, right sides facing. Press the seam open and neaten the edges.
5. Turn and make an elastic casing on the waist edge, folding on the line marked on the pattern (see page 12 for making casings and inserting elastic).
6. Make a narrow turned-under hem on the Shorts' legs (see page 14).

Making the Top

1. The selvedges on the Centre Backs mean that no stitching or neatening is required. Pin Front to Backs on the shoulder seams, right sides of fabric facing. Baste and then machine-stitch. Press seams open and neaten edges.

Neckline

2. Following the technique described on page 11 for applying bias strips, bind the neckline, leaving the binding ends free at Back neck for making ties.
3. Fold, press and machine-stitch the binding ties, neatening the ends with hand-sewing.

Side seams

4. Turn a double, narrow hem on the edges of the Front and Back (Fig 2). Topstitch 6mm *(¼in)* from the edge.
5. Measure and mark the position of the side seam as shown in Fig 2. With right sides facing, machine-stitch the side seams.

Hem

6. Make a turned-under hem on the bottom edge to the desired length (see page 14 for technique).

Fancy dress

Little boys and girls love dressing up, and the Waistcoat Suit pattern on the previous page makes a good cowboy outfit.

Make the waistcoat in a bright, red cotton fabric and appliqué a yellow, sheriff's star to the front.

Make the trousers in yellow cotton and sew cotton fringing to the side seams.

Apply two red patches to the trouser knees and make a neckerchief from a scrap of fabric.

Winter overtop

By reversing the Sun Set Top pattern, so that the opening is at the front, a useful winter-warmer can be made.

Use fleecy fabric or a soft woollen fabric. Stitch ties to the front, or a large, decorative hook and eye.

Fig 1   selvedge   selvedge

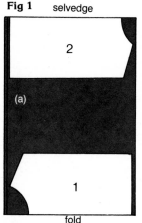
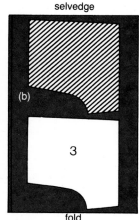

Fig 1 *Fabric layouts for the Sun Set: (a) printed fabric, (b) white fabric*

Fig 2 *Turn a double, narrow hem on the edges of the Front and Back, then topstitch 6mm (¼in) from the edge*

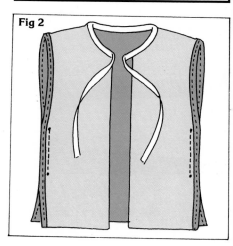

Stripy one-piece

This all-in-one is just the sort of 'fun' outfit children love to wear. It is fully lined and has press-on fasteners at the shoulders for quick dressing – and undressing.

Materials required

To fit sizes chest 58-60cm (23-24in), inside leg length 42cm (16½in)
Pattern piece Main piece 1
2m *(2¼yd)* of 120cm *(48in)*-wide

plain cotton fabric
2m *(2¼yd)* of 120cm *(48in)*-wide striped cotton fabric
4 press-on fasteners
Matching sewing thread
Alternative fabrics Seersucker, poplin, lightweight denim

Preparation

Fig 1 is the graph pattern for the One-piece. The scale is 1 square=5cm *(2in)* and two sizes are given on the pattern, the smaller size indicated in a coloured line. A seam allowance of 1cm *(⅜in)* is included on all pattern pieces.

Draw the pattern to scale on squared pattern paper. Cut out the pieces, copying in all markings.

Following the fabric layout (Fig 2), pin the pattern piece to each of the fabrics. Cut out 4 pieces from the plain fabric and 4 pieces from the striped fabric. Transfer all markings to fabric.

Making the One-piece

1. Pin 1 striped piece and 1 plain piece together on the Centre Front seam (A–B on the pattern). Baste and then machine-stitch the seam. Clip into the curve, press the seam open and neaten edges. This is the Front.
2. Reversing the order of striped/plain, pin 1 plain and 1 striped together on the Centre Front seam and make up as for the Front. This is the Back.

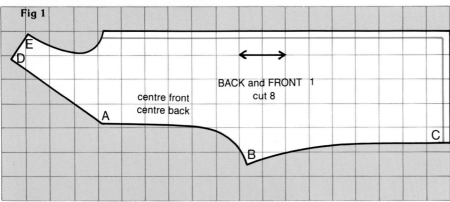

Fig 1

centre front
centre back

BACK and FRONT   1
cut 8

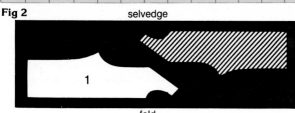

Fig 2

selvedge

1

fold

Fig 1 *Graph pattern for the Stripy One-piece, 1sq = 5cm (2in)*

Fig 2 *Fabric layout for plain and striped fabrics*

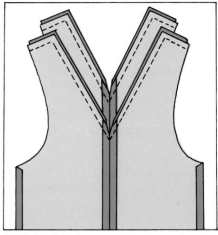

Fig 3 *Clip into the seam at Centre Front and Centre Back*

3. Pin and baste Front to Back on the inside leg seams. Machine-stitch from the leg hem through the crotch to the other leg hem in one operation (C−B−C on the pattern). Clip into the curves and press open the seam. Neaten the edges (see page 9 for reducing fabric bulk in crossed seams).

4. Pin and baste the side seams, then machine-stitch. Press seams open and neaten the edges.

Making the lining

5. Follow stages 1-4 to make the lining, reversing the order of striped and plain fabric.

6. With right sides of fabric together, pin the lining to the garment around the neckline and straps (E−D−A−D−E on the pattern).

7. Baste and then machine-stitch. Trim the seam allowance back to 6mm *(¼in)* and clip into the seam at the 'v' on Centre Front and Centre Back (Fig 3).

8. Turn the garment to the right side and press.

9. Make a 6mm *(¼in)* turning to the inside of the garment on the armhole edges. Press, then baste the edges together. Machine-stitch, close to the edges.

10. Make a 6mm *(¼in)* turning to the inside of the garment on the trouser hems. Press and baste the edges together. Machine-stitch, close to the edges.

11. Apply two press-on fasteners to each of the shoulders (see picture).

Sunday best

This drop-waisted dress has the bodice and sleeves cut in one for easy sewing. A lace neck-frill and satin ribbon sash make a simple style very special.

Materials required

To fit sizes chest 58-60cm (23-24in), length shoulder to hem 67cm (26½in)
Pattern pieces Bodice Front 1, Bodice Back 2. Cut 2 Skirt pieces from fabric
1.70m *(1⅞yd)* of 120cm *(48in)*-wide Swiss-dotted poly/cotton lawn
80cm *(31in)* of 8cm *(3¼in)*-wide lace edging (or strips cut from all-over lace)
1m *(1⅛yd)* of 5cm *(2in)*-wide double face polyester satin ribbon
Matching sewing thread
Alternative fabrics Seersucker, polyester crepe-de-chine, printed poly/cotton

Preparation

Fig 1 is the graph pattern for the Bodice pieces. The scale is 1 square=5cm *(2in)* and two sizes are given, the smaller size indicated in a coloured line. A seam allowance of 1cm *(⅜in)* is included on the pattern.

Draw the pattern to scale on squared pattern paper. Cut out the pieces, copying in all markings.

Following the fabric layout (Fig 2), cut out 2 Skirt pieces from the fabric on the fold. Each Skirt piece measures 108×41cm *(42½×16½in)*. Pin the Bodice pieces in position and cut out 1 Bodice Front on the fold of fabric and 2 Backs.

From remaining fabric, cut a bias strip 40×3cm *(16×1¼in)* for binding the neck edge.

Cut 2 bias strips 30×3cm *(12×1¼in)* for Back neck ties.

Making the Dress
Skirt

1. Pin the 2 Skirt pieces together, right sides facing, on the short, side seam edges.
2. Baste and then machine-stitch the seams. Press seams open and neaten the edges.
3. Gather the top edge of the skirt (see page 10 for technique). Leave the gathering threads wound on pins as described.
Bodice
4. Pin the 2 Backs together on the Centre Back seam, between the marks A−B (on the pattern). Baste and machine-stitch the seam. Press

the seam open and neaten the edges.
5. Above the mark A, press the seam allowances to the wrong side for a Back neck opening. Neaten the edges and then topstitch 3mm *(⅛in)* from the fold.
6. Pin the Bodice Front to Back on the shoulder seams. Baste and then machine-stitch. Press seam allowances open and neaten the edges.
7. Pin and baste the side and underarm seams. Machine-stitch, right sides facing, in one operation. Clip into the curves for ease. Press the seam open and neaten the edges

Joining Bodice to Skirt

8. Pull up the gathers to fit the skirt to the bodice (see page 10 for technique).
9. Pin Skirt to Bodice, right sides facing and setting pins vertically.
10. Stitch Skirt to Bodice. Press the seam towards the skirt, trim back the seam allowances to 6mm *(¼in)* and zigzag-stitch the seam edges together to neaten.

Collar

11. Make a narrow turning on the short ends of the lace strip and zigzag-stitch.
12. Gather the lace to fit the neckline and baste to the right side.
13. Prepare the bias strip of fabric for binding the neckline. Bind the neck edge and hand-sew the Back neck edges to neaten (see page 11 for techniques).

Ties

14. Fold and machine-stitch the ties strips to make rouleau (see page 13 for technique).

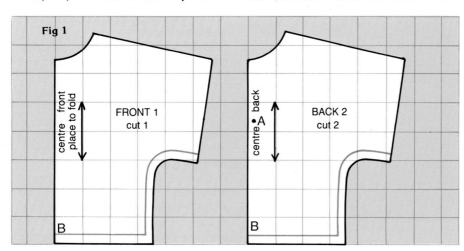

Fig 1

centre front
place to fold

FRONT 1
cut 1

B

centre back

•A

BACK 2
cut 2

B

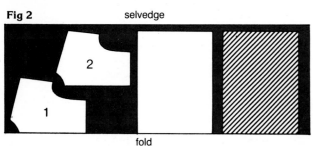

Fig 2   selvedge

2

1

fold

Fig 1 *Graph pattern for the dress Bodice pieces, 1sq = 5cm (2in)*

Fig 2 *Fabric layout for the dress pattern pieces*

Fig 3 *Sew the ribbon to the side seam, positioning it across the bodice and skirt seam*

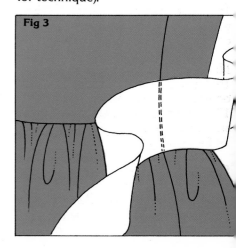

Fig 3

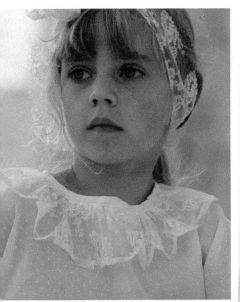

15. Neaten one end of each rouleau with hand-sewing. Hand-sew the other end to the Back neck for ties.

Hems

16. Make narrow turned-under hems on the sleeves edges.
17. Make a turned-under hem on the skirt to the desired length (see page 14 for technique).

Sash

18. Fold the ribbon in two across the middle. Hand-sew the fold to the side seam, positioning it halfway across the bodice and skirt seam (Fig 3).

Fun and fashion

Children enjoy wearing decorations on their clothes — embroidered motifs on shirts, jeans, skirts and suits. Purchased character motifs are simple to apply and the techniques for doing this are on page 17.

Here are some motifs that can be used for appliqué or embroidery — or they can be painted with fabric paints directly on to the garment pieces. Trace the motifs, then transfer them to the fabric with dressmakers' carbon paper.